William Shakespeare's

The
Tempest

Text by
Corinna Siebert Ruth
(M.A., California State University-Fresno)
Department of English
Kings River Community College
Reedley, California

Illustrations by
Karen Pica

Research & Education Association

Dr. M. Fogiel, Director

MAXnotes® for
THE TEMPEST

Printed in the United States of America

Library of Congress Control Number 2001094422

International Standard Book Number 0-87891-052-2

MAXnotes® is a registered trademark of
Research & Education Association, Piscataway, New Jersey 08854

What **MAXnotes**® *Will Do for You*

This book is intended to help you absorb the essential contents and features of William Shakespeare's *The Tempest* and to help you gain a thorough understanding of the work. Our book has been designed to do this more quickly and effectively than any other study guide.

For best results, this **MAXnotes** book should be used as a companion to the actual work, not instead of it. The interaction between the two will greatly benefit you.

To help you in your studies, this book presents the most up-to-date interpretations of every section of the actual work, followed by questions and fully explained answers that will enable you to analyze the material critically. The questions also will help you to test your understanding of the work and will prepare you for discussions and exams.

Meaningful illustrations are included to further enhance your understanding and enjoyment of the literary work. The illustrations are designed to place you into the mood and spirit of the work's settings.

The **MAXnotes** also include summaries, character lists, explanations of plot, and section-by-section analyses. A biography of the author and discussion of the work's historical context will help you put this literary piece into the proper perspective of what is taking place.

The use of this study guide will save you the hours of preparation time that would ordinarily be required to arrive at a complete grasp of this work of literature. You will be well-prepared for classroom discussions, homework, and exams. The guidelines that are included for writing papers and reports on various topics will prepare you for any added work which may be assigned.

The **MAXnotes** will take your grades "to the max."

Dr. Max Fogiel
Program Director

Contents

> **Each chapter includes List of Characters, Summary, Analysis, Study Questions and Answers, and Suggested Essay Topics.**

MAXnotes® are simply the best – but don't just take our word for it...

"... I have told every bookstore in the area to carry your MAXnotes. They are the only notes I recommend to my students. There is no comparison between MAXnotes and all other notes ..."
    – High School Teacher & Reading Specialist, Arlington High School, Arlington, MA

"... I discovered the MAXnotes when a friend loaned me her copy of the *MAXnotes for Romeo and Juliet*. The book really helped me understand the story. Please send me a list of stores in my area that carry the MAXnotes. I would like to use more of them ..."
    – Student, San Marino, CA

"... The two MAXnotes titles that I have used have been very, very useful in helping me understand the subject matter reviewed. Thank you for creating the MAXnotes series ..."
    – Student, Morrisville, PA

A Glance at Some of the Characters

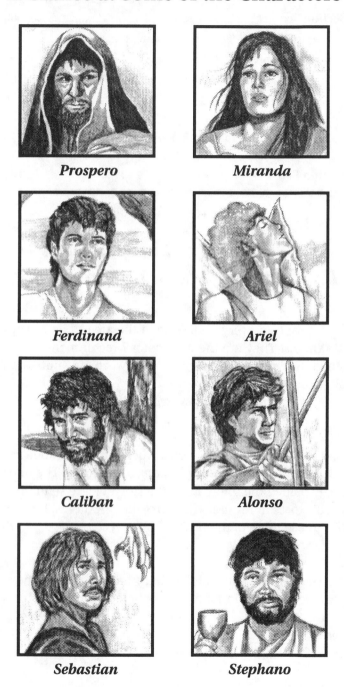

Prospero

Miranda

Ferdinand

Ariel

Caliban

Alonso

Sebastian

Stephano

Introduction

The Life and Work of William Shakespeare

The details of William Shakespeare's life are sketchy, mostly mere surmise based upon court or other clerical records. His parents, John and Mary (Arden), were married about 1557; she was of the landed gentry, and he was a yeoman—a glover and commodities merchant. By 1568, John had risen through the ranks of town government and held the position of high bailiff, which was a position similar to mayor. William, the eldest son and the third of eight children, was born in 1564, probably on April 23, several days before his baptism on April 26 in Stratford-upon-Avon. Shakespeare is also believed to have died on the same date—April 23—in 1616.

It is believed that William attended the local grammar school in Stratford where his parents lived, and that he studied primarily Latin, rhetoric, logic, and literature. Shakespeare probably left school at age 15, which was the norm, to take a job, especially since this was the period of his father's financial difficulty. At age 18 (1582), William married Anne Hathaway, a local farmer's daughter who was eight years his senior. Their first daughter (Susanna) was born six months later (1583), and twins Judith and Hamnet were born in 1585.

Shakespeare's life can be divided into three periods: the first 20 years in Stratford, which include his schooling, early marriage, and fatherhood; the next 25 years as an actor and playwright in London; and the last five in retirement in Stratford where he enjoyed moderate wealth gained from his theatrical successes. The years linking the first two periods are marked by a lack of information about Shakespeare, and are often referred to as the "dark years."

At some point during the "dark years," Shakespeare began his career with a London theatrical company, perhaps in 1589, for he was already an actor and playwright of some note by 1592. Shakespeare apparently wrote and acted for numerous theatrical companies, including Pembroke's Men, and Strange's Men, which later became the Chamberlain's Men, with whom he remained for the rest of his career.

In 1592, the Plague closed the theaters for about two years, and Shakespeare turned to writing book-length narrative poetry. Most notable were "Venus and Adonis" and "The Rape of Lucrece," both of which were dedicated to the Earl of Southampton, whom scholars accept as Shakespeare's friend and benefactor despite a lack of documentation. During this same period, Shakespeare was writing his sonnets, which are more likely signs of the time's fashion rather than actual love poems detailing any particular relationship. He returned to playwriting when theaters reopened in 1594, and did not continue to write poetry. His sonnets were published without his consent in 1609, shortly before his retirement.

Amid all of his success, Shakespeare suffered the loss of his only son, Hamnet, who died in 1596 at the age of 11. But Shakespeare's career continued unabated, and in London in 1599, he became one of the partners in the new Globe Theater, which was built by the Chamberlain's Men.

Shakespeare wrote very little after 1612, which was the year he completed *Henry VIII.* It was during a performance of this play in 1613 that the Globe caught fire and burned to the ground. Sometime between 1610 and 1613, Shakespeare returned to Stratford, where he owned a large house and property, to spend his remaining years with his family.

William Shakespeare died on April 23, 1616, and was buried two days later in the chancel of Holy Trinity Church, where he had been baptized exactly 52 years earlier. His literary legacy included 37 plays, 154 sonnets and five major poems.

Incredibly, most of Shakespeare's plays had never been published in anything except pamphlet form, and were simply extant as acting scripts stored at the Globe. Theater scripts were not regarded as literary works of art, but only the basis for the performance. Plays were simply a popular form of entertainment for all layers of society in Shakespeare's time. Only the efforts of two of Shakespeare's company, John Heminges and Henry Condell, preserved his 36 plays (minus *Pericles,* the thirty-seventh).

Historical Background

Most of Shakespeare's comedies, histories, and tragedies were written during England's "golden age" under the celebrated 45-year reign (1558-1603) of Queen Elizabeth I. Historically, the Elizabethan era took place in the wake of the Protestant Reformation when the English Renaissance was ushered in and the arts flourished. When King James I succeeded Elizabeth to the throne after her death in 1603, he continued, at least to some extent, the rich cultural legacy left by the late queen. The new king, a patron of the arts, agreed to sponsor the King's Men, Shakespeare's theatrical group.

By 1608, after an illustrious career as a playwright, Shakespeare turned away from the great tragedies (*Hamlet, Othello,* and *King Lear*) and directed his creative energies toward the romances or tragi-comedies (*The Tempest, Pericles, Cymbeline,* and *The Winter's Tale*).

The romances involve improbable and fanciful events that border on imagination rather than fact. Prospero's magic is typical of the genre. Characters are often drawn in opposing categories of black and white and include the idealized heroine. In *The Tempest,* for example, Miranda is portrayed as the pure image of chastity. Love in the romances is characteristically subjected to great difficulty. Miranda stands by anxiously as she watches Ferdinand bear the "trials of love" imposed upon him by Prospero.

The Tempest is tragi-comic with a serious plot that could be suitable for tragedy but ends happily like a comedy. The usurpation of Prospero's dukedom and the plot of Antonio and Sebastian to kill Alonso and Gonzalo carry potential tragic elements, but the evil plans are eventually thwarted, and all ends happily.

The Tempest was first published in the Folio edition of 1623 where it was placed as the opening work. According to an account book at the Revel's Office in Somerset House, the play was first performed at Whitehall on Hallowmas night, November 1, 1611. It was produced in court for the second time to celebrate the marriage of the daughter of James I, Princess Elizabeth, to the Elector Palatine in the winter of 1612-13.

There are no known sources for the main plot, but it is believed that Shakespeare used Strachey's *True Repertory of the Wrack and Redemption of Sir Thomas Gates* (dated July 15, 1610 and later published in *Purchas His Pilgrims* in 1625), Jourdain's *A Discovery of the Bermudas* (published 1610), and the Virginia Council's *True Declaration of the Estate of the Colony in Virginia* (published 1610). These publications are an account of the Virginia Company Expedition from Plymouth to Jamestown. News reached England that all except the flagship, *The Sea Adventure*, had arrived safely. It was rumored that the admiral, Sir George Somers, and the future governor of Virginia, Sir Thomas Gates, had drowned in a storm at sea. To everyone's surprise, the two men miraculously appeared in Jamestown with the story that they had run aground on the isle of Bermuda. For the character of Caliban, Shakespeare also used Montaigne's essay, "Of the Cannibals," which praised the savage of the New World as the natural man. Since these sources are dated as late as 1610, Shakespeare could not have written the play much before it was performed in 1611.

Shakespeare's new genre in his last plays was well-received by his early seventeenth-century audience and the public's new interest did, in fact, reach far beyond to the end of the century with Shadwell's tragi-comedy, *Royal Shepherdess*, and Dryden's *Secret Love*.

The abundance of literary criticism on *The Tempest* dates back to the eighteenth century when Dr. Samuel Johnson apologizes for Shakespeare's use of song. He feels that Ariel's songs "express nothing great." Coleridge praises the play for its morality, though he feels that Shakespeare "may sometimes be gross." G. Wilson Knight approaches the play with a theme of immortality which is metaphorically expressed in terms of victorious love. Bordering on the allegorical, Knight's view equates the sea to fortune, the tempests to children and birth, and gentleness to royal blood. For W. L. Godschalk, the central thrust of the play lies in the problems of government rather than the progress of the soul toward redemption.

Kermode's thematic approach to *The Tempest* concerns the opposition between the worlds of Prospero's art and Caliban's nature. Zimbardo deals with the universal conflict between order and chaos, asserting that Prospero's art is an attempt at imposing form on the formless. She places Caliban at the center of disorder, conceding, however, that he too feels the effect of the harmony or order of the island but just for a moment. Reflecting the literary criticism of the nineteenth century, James Russell Lowell sees the play as an allegory in which Prospero represents imagination, Ariel is seen as fancy, and Caliban as brute understanding. Nutall, though an allegorist, rejects Lowell's nineteenth-century view. He sees *The Tempest* as a metaphysical allegory in which Ariel and Caliban could be the psychic processes.

In contrast to the allegorists who have idealized Prospero as Shakespeare himself, Cutts would have us believe that Prospero is out for revenge, selfishly seeking his own end which is the restoration of his power. Unlike Cutts, Northrop Frye contrasts Prospero's "white magic" with the "black magic" of Sycorax. Prospero's motives are good, he reasons, and in tune with the higher order of nature. Sisson also feels that in view of Parliament's statute against witchcraft and the conjuration of evil spirits, Shakespeare would have been careful to make a sharp distinction between the evil powers of Sycorax representing "black magic" and the "white magic" of Prospero which does not deal with incantations in the performance of magic.

Master List of Characters

Prospero—*the rightful Duke of Milan whose dukedom has been usurped by his brother Antonio. Prospero controls the island and its inhabitants with a God-like power.*

Miranda—*Prospero's fifteen-year-old daughter who has been living with him on the island since their banishment from Milan when she was only three years old. Her father and Caliban are the only humans she remembers. When she meets Ferdinand, she falls in love with him almost immediately and innocently* *offers herself to him as his wife.*

Ferdinand—*He is the son of Alonso, King of Naples. Though he is a man of royal blood, he must endure the dishonor of carrying logs for Prospero as a trial of his love for Miranda.*

Ariel—*an airy spirit who has suffered a twelve-year imprisonment in a "cloven pine" for refusing the "earthy and abhorr'd commands" of the evil witch, Sycorax. Prospero releases Ariel, only to subject him to further servitude. With the aid of Prospero, Ariel conjures up the tempest and performs other acts of magic throughout the play. Prospero finally gives him his freedom at the end.*

Caliban—*Prospero refers to him as a "born devil" whose mother was the evil witch, Sycorax. He is a deformed monster whose bestial nature cannot be changed, though he has been taught to speak a language. Paradoxically, Caliban usually speaks in verse and is given some of the most poetic lines in the play.*

Alonso—*Ferdinand's father, the King of Naples, who grieves over the supposed loss of his son. He is bearing a double loss since he recently lost his daughter, Claribel, in marriage to the King of Tunis. He has been instrumental in the usurpation of Prospero's Dukedom but is repentant and, thereby, regenerated by the end of the play.*

Antonio—*Prospero's brother, the usurping Duke of Milan, who helps Sebastian plot the death of his own brother, the King of Naples.*

Sebastian—*Alonso's brother whose gullibility leads him to look up to Antonio as his model. Just as Antonio has usurped his brother Prospero as the rightful Duke of Milan, Sebastian also wishes to take Alonso's place as the King of Naples.*

Gonzalo—*An old councilor whose loyalty to the king poses a threat to Antonio and Sebastian in their plot of regicide.*

Stephano—*Alonso's "drunken butler" who considers himself superior to Trinculo. Electing Stephano as his own "noble lord" and the new king of the island, Caliban kneels at Stephano's feet. Adding to the incongruity, Caliban helps to plot Prospero's death so that Stephano can take his place as king of the island.*

Trinculo—*the king's jester who is Stephano's constant companion. He jeers at Caliban's newly-acquired devotion to Stephano as the future lord of the island.*

Adrian and Francisco—*two lords who are in attendance with Alonso's royal party but are given little characterization by Shakespeare.*

Boatswain—*the ship's officer in charge of the deck crew, the rigging, and the cables. He is efficient and confident as he orders the king to stay out of his way and "keep below" in the cabins.*

Iris, Ceres, Juno, Nymphs, and Reapers—*spirits who perform the wedding masque for Ferdinand and Miranda.*

Summary of the Play

Prospero, the rightful Duke of Milan, has been living on a primitive island with his fifteen-year-old daughter, Miranda, for the past 12 years. His dukedom had been usurped by his own brother, Antonio, whom Prospero had entrusted to manage the affairs of government while he was concentrating on his study of the liberal arts. With the support of Alonso, the King of Naples, Antonio conspired against his brother to become the new Duke of Milan. Prospero and his three-year-old daughter were put on "a rotten carcass of a butt" without a sail. Gonzalo, a member of the king's council, took pity on them, and stocked the leaky vessel with food, fresh water, clothing, and Prospero's books. Providence has now brought his enemies to the shore of the island, and Prospero must act quickly.

The action begins with a tempestuous storm at sea. Afraid for their lives, Alonso and Gonzalo urge the Boatswain to do all he can to save the ship, but he rudely orders the royal party to stay in their cabins and "trouble us not." They are finally convinced to go below and pray for mercy.

Ariel, an airy spirit, raised the tempest just as he was instructed by Prospero, his master, informing Prospero that all except the mariners plunged into the sea. Ariel reports that he has left the ship safely docked in the harbor with the mariners aboard. The rest of

the passengers, with garments unblemished, have been dispersed
around the island. Ariel then lures Ferdinand, Prince of Naples,
onto the island with his songs, informing him of his father's supposed death by drowning. The young prince is led past Prospero's
cave where he meets Miranda, and they fall in love. To keep
Ferdinand from winning his prize (Miranda) too quickly and easily, Prospero uses his magic to force Ferdinand to yield to the in-
dignity of stacking logs.

Elsewhere on the island, Ariel, with the help of Prospero's
magic, puts Alonso and Gonzalo to sleep. While they sleep Antonio and Sebastian conspire to kill Alonso and Gonzalo and take
over the throne. Just as they draw their swords, Ariel awakens
Gonzalo and he, in turn, rouses the king. The conspirators claim
that they heard wild animals and drew their swords. The king
readily accepts their excuse.

Caliban enters, cursing his master, Prospero, for enslaving him.
Trinculo, the king's jester, appears, hiding under Caliban's cloak to
escape a rainstorm. Stephano approaches them, thinking it is a
monster with four legs. He finally recognizes Trinculo and is sur-
prised to see him alive. Stephano, having drifted ashore on a barrel of wine, offers Caliban a drink. Unaccustomed to the effects of
the alcohol, Caliban kneels to Stephano, taking him for a god who
"bears celestial liquor." Determined that Stephano should be lord
of the island, Caliban leads the pair to Prospero's cave where they
plan to murder him.

Prospero magically sets a banquet for the royal party, but Ariel,
disguised as a harpy, claps his wings over the table, and it vanishes.
Ariel warns the royal party that the storm was a punishment for
their foul deeds, and there is no way out except repentance. In
another part of the island, Prospero relieves Ferdinand of his duties, telling him he has endured the difficult trial of love and has
won Miranda's hand in marriage. Ariel arranges a masque in honor
of the happy couple, but while the masque is in progress, Prospero
suddenly remembers Caliban's plot to kill him, and the masque
vanishes. Ariel has lead the conspirators from the filthy-mantled
pool to Prospero's "glistering apparel" hanging on a lime tree in
front of his cave. Though Caliban is annoyed, his companions are
gleefully sidetracked, stealing the royal robes and forgetting their

purpose at hand which is to murder Prospero. Finally, spirits in the shape of dogs are released, and the thieving trio are driven out.

The king and his party are brought to Prospero where he charms them in his magic circle, praising Gonzalo for his kindness, but censuring Alonso for his cruelty and Antonio for his ambition. Removing his magician's robe, Prospero gives up his magic powers, presenting himself to Alonso as the "wronged Duke of Milan," and the repentant king immediately restores his dukedom. In a sudden spirit of forgiveness, he pardons all of them for their crimes against him. He then leads Alonso to his cell where Ferdinand and Miranda are making a pretense of playing chess. Alonso is overjoyed to see his son alive.

Ariel enters with the master and boatswain of the ship. To the king's amazement the ship is undamaged and docked in the harbor. The three conspirators, driven by Ariel, appear in their stolen royal apparel. Caliban calls himself a "thrice-double ass" to have taken Stephano for a god. Prospero invites the king's entire party to spend the night in his cell where he will give them an account of his last 12 years on the island. In the morning they will return to Naples where they will prepare for the marriage of the betrothed pair, Ferdinand and Miranda.

Prospero rewards Ariel for his services by giving him his freedom and releasing him to the elements. In the epilogue Prospero tells the audience his magic powers are gone, his dukedom has been restored, and he has forgiven his enemies. He now asks them to praise his performance with their applause and, thereby, release him from the illusory world of the island.

Estimated Reading Time

Most Shakespeare plays, written to be viewed by an audience, usually take approximately three hours to perform on the stage. *The Tempest* is an unusually short play with a performance time of about two hours. It would be possible to read it almost as fast the first time around to get the plot of the story. *The Tempest* is impressive theater with its magical manipulations, its masque, including spirit-like goddesses, its spirits in the form of dogs, and, perhaps above all, its songs. For this reason an auditory tape of *The Tempest,* available at most university or county libraries, is an excellent device that can be used to follow along with the text, making the drama more interesting by bringing the characters alive with the use of sound effects. After the initial reading, it should be read more carefully, taking special note of the difficult words and phrases that are glossed at the bottom of most Shakespeare texts. This reading would probably take about 4-5 hours for the entire play, allowing a little less than an hour for each of the five acts. Since the acts of *The Tempest* vary from one to three scenes each, the length of reading time for each act will, of course, vary. It should be noted that the length of the scenes also varies from 63 to 504 lines.

SECTION TWO

Act I

Act I, Scene 1

New Characters:

Alonso: *king of Naples who has conspired to usurp Prospero's duke-dom*

Gonzalo: *an old councilor who has shown compassion to Prospero and Miranda*

Antonio: *Prospero's brother, the usurping Duke of Milan*

Sebastian: *Alonso's brother*

Ship–master: *master or captain of the ship*

Boatswain: *the ship's officer in charge of the crew and the rigging of the sails*

Mariners: *the ship's crew who take orders from the Boatswain*

Summary

The play begins with flashes of lightning, the cracking of thunder, and the urgent shouts of the Ship–master, ordering the Boat-swain to mobilize his crew and prevent the ship from running aground. The Boatswain responds promptly, commanding his men to "take in the topsail" and prepare for the storm at sea. The sway-ing of the ship drives its royal passengers to the top deck in fear. Alonso and Antonio do not immediately see the master of the ship and assume he is shirking his duty. They urge the Boatswain to prod his men into action. The scurrilous Boatswain minces no words, ordering the royal party to stay in their cabins. He reminds Alonso that even the king has no authority over the raging sea, and he is only hindering them from doing their job.

Gonzalo finds comfort in his belief that the Boatswain is the kind of impudent fellow who was born to be hanged and, consequently, will not drown. Sebastian and Antonio curse the Boatswain, but he rudely challenges them to do the job themselves if they are not satisfied. Alonso and Ferdinand finally go below and the rest of the royal party join them to pray for mercy after the mariners arrive with news that all is lost.

Analysis

It has been suggested that the title of the play should be *The Island* rather than *The Tempest* since the storm at sea takes place only in the first scene. Some critics believe, however, that the tempest pervades the entire play, having caused the suffering of Prospero's enemies which continues long after the storm has abated. Alonso suffers grief for his lost son throughout most of the play. By the end, Ferdinand has been found, Alonso's sin against Prospero has been forgiven, and his inner tempest subsides. He has been purified through his suffering. The storm at sea is brought about by Prospero's magic which permeates the actions of the characters until Act V when he removes his magician's robe. It is only then that its purpose has been accomplished. His dukedom has been restored and his enemies forgiven.

In the opening scene, set aboard a ship in a storm-tossed sea, it is immediately apparent that a hierarchy exists among the ship's officers and crew consisting of the Ship-master, the Boatswain, and the mariners. This maritime society is a microcosm of the larger hierarchical society made up of the king, the noblemen, and the common people. In a social and political society the king would normally exercise his authority over all of his people, but on the ship at sea he has entered the domain of the Ship-master and Boatswain and must now succumb to their authority. They are the ones who hold the king's very life in their hands. As the Boatswain so aptly puts it: "What cares these roarers for the name of king?" The king is not more powerful than the roaring sea. This idea foreshad-

ows the image in Ariel's song, "Full Fadom Five,"in Act I, Scene 2 in which he asserts that Alonso "doth suffer a sea-change." Though Alonso does not actually die as the song suggests, the image is symbolic of the change he will go through on the island.

In retaliation for the Boatswain's rude manners, Gonzalo persists in repeating a joke about him. The old councilor finds comfort in the fact that he "sees no drowning mark upon him (the Boatswain)" since he is destined to be hanged. Gonzalo insists that the passengers "make the rope of his destiny our cable." If the Boatswain's destiny points to the gallows, it is reasonable that he will not meet his death by drowning at sea and, in that case, neither will any of the other passengers. Neil H. Wright has noted that the symbolic "rope is a hangman's noose for the Boatswain but a saving cable for the crew and passengers" (Neil H. Wright, "Reality and Illusion as a Philosophical Pattern in *The Tempest*," 249). Ironically, Gonzalo's joke is a prophetic statement since everyone on the ship eventually reaches the shore safely.

When the mariners report that all is lost, Sebastian, Antonio, and Gonzalo are finally convinced of the seriousness of the situation. They decide to go below and join Alonso and Ferdinand in their prayers. Soon a confusing noise is heard, and Gonzalo, thinking they have run aground on a rock, shouts "We split, we split, we split." Antonio suggests that they "sink wi' th' king," but Sebastian would rather "take leave of him." Sebastian's statement foreshadows his conspiracy to kill his brother, the king, later in the play.

Study Questions

1. Who was in charge of the ship during the storm at sea?

2. Why did Alonso, the king, interfere with the Boatswain's work in securing the ship during the storm?

3. Where did the Boatswain tell the king and his courtiers to go?

4. Who were the first to go to their cabins below the top deck?

5. What joke does Gonzalo tell concerning the Boatswain?

6. How does this joke affect the rest of the passengers and crew?

7. How do Sebastian and Antonio react to the Boatswain?

8. How does the Boatswain respond to Sebastian's and Antonio's insulting remarks?

9. How does Antonio decide to die in the storm at sea?

10. How loyal is Sebastian to his brother, the king?

Answers

1. The Ship–master was in charge of the Boatswain and the mariners.

2. The king was accustomed to being the supreme authority.

3. The Boatswain told the king and his courtiers to go to their cabins below.

4. Alonso, the king, and Ferdinand, the prince, were the first to go below and pray.

5. Gonzalo's joke implies that the Boatswain was born to be hanged and need not fear drowning.

6. If the Boatswain does not drown, the rest of the passengers and crew will also be spared.

7. Sebastian and Antonio curse the Boatswain and call him names.

8. The Boatswain responds with "work you then" if they don't like the way he is handling the job.

9. Antonio wants to sink into the sea with the king.

10. Sebastian wants to leave the king when he thinks the ship is sinking.

Suggested Essay Topics

1. With disrespect for the king, the Boatswain says, "What cares these roarers for the name of king?" Explicate this passage in the light of the king's authority at sea. To whose authority did the king succumb? Did the Boatswain have power over the king? Cite examples from the play to support your answer.

2. Gonzalo keeps a sense of humor in spite of the chaos of the

storm. Write an essay explaining his joke concerning the
Boatswain. Why did he think the Boatswain was the kind of
fellow who was born to be hanged? Why would that keep
him from drowning? What effect would the Boatswain's fate
have on the other passengers and crew? Draw your examples
from the play to support your ideas.

Act I, Scene 2, lines 1-188

New Characters:

Prospero: *the rightful Duke of Milan whose dukedom has been
usurped by his brother, Antonio*

Miranda: *Prospero's fifteen-year-old daughter*

Summary

The scene is set on an island at the mouth of Prospero's cave
where he and Miranda have been living for the past 12 years. From
the shore they have been watching the sinking ship and listening
to the heartrending cries of the people on board. Aware that her
father has raised the tempest with his magic, Miranda begs him to
calm the "wild waters" and end the suffering. Prospero assures her
that no harm has been done, and that he has acted solely on her
behalf.

He expresses his regret that she is ignorant of her true station
in life. Moreover, she does not know that he is a man of high rank.
She admits that the idea has not occurred to her. Convinced that
the time is now right, Prospero begins the account of their precarious voyage to the island when she was not quite three years
old. He asks her whether she has any memory of her life before
she came to the island. She replies that she can remember four or
five women who tended her, but has no recollection of her arrival
at the island with her father. He goes on to explain that he is the
rightful Duke of Milan whose dukedom had been usurped by his
own brother, Antonio, who had been entrusted to manage the affairs of state so that Prospero could be free to concentrate on his
"secret studies." With both money and power at his constant dis-

posal, Antonio began to believe that he was actually the duke.

Interspersed into his lengthy exposition are Prospero's occasional accusations against Miranda for not listening. He then goes on to explain that the King of Naples had been his long-lasting enemy. In exchange for Antonio's homage and tribute, the king levied an army, removed Prospero from his rightful position as duke and replaced him with Antonio, the new Duke of Milan. At midnight, Prospero and Miranda were hurried aboard a rotten tub without a sail and left alone on the roaring sea. Miranda asks her father why Alonso and Antonio did not have them killed immediately. Prospero explains that they did not dare because of his people's love for him as Duke of Milan. The conspirators decided instead to make Prospero's death look like an accident. Out of compassion for Prospero and Miranda, Gonzalo packed the rotting vessel with food, water, clothing, and an ample supply of books from Prospero's library. He tells Miranda that, with her own father as her tutor, she has been fortunate to have a better schoolmaster than most princesses.

Prospero's long discourse has solved many mysteries for Miranda, but she still wonders why her father has raised the storm at sea. He tells her it has been his good fortune that his enemies have accidentally wandered to the shore of this island, and he must act now, or he might never be given another chance. Dressing in his magic robe, he puts Miranda into a deep sleep and signals Ariel to approach.

Analysis

One of the major themes in *The Tempest* is illusion versus reality as it relates to the opposing worlds of a primitive island and the civilized culture of Milan. The storm at sea seems to be endangering the lives of its passengers and crew, but when Miranda begs her father to allay the "wild waters," he calms her fears, telling her there has been "no harm done." We learn later that the "brave vessel" has not been "dash'd all to pieces," as Miranda had feared, but rests safely in the harbor.

The magical atmosphere of the island, with its primeval surroundings, is Prospero's realm. While he was still in Milan, he became increasingly "transported and rapt in secret studies." He kept

moving further into his illusory world of books which was in stark contrast to the management of his dukedom in the real world of Milan. Ironically, Antonio, who had been entrusted to administer the affairs of government for Prospero, also lived under the illusion that "he was indeed the duke." His royalty was only an "outward face," but his ambition grew, and, with the help of Alonso, the king, he conspired against Prospero to become the Duke of Milan.

Writing in the consciousness of his own age, Shakespeare's view of the natural order was based on the hierarchy of all beings and things. The idea had its beginnings with Plato and Aristotle and influenced the ethics of medieval thought which extended well into the sixteenth century and beyond. In the hierarchy, God was supreme and all other beings had a superior to whom they owed obedience and an inferior whom they ruled. It extended from God to the lowest animals and even to inanimate objects. When the hierarchy was destroyed, disorder and chaos reigned. All would go well as long as individuals in families and the larger society knew their place. Antonio's selfish refusal to recognize his particular place in the social and political hierarchy resulted in the overthrow of Prospero's dukedom and the consequent corruption of the natural harmony. Antonio's subversiveness led to anarchy in the state and violated the trust between brothers as well. Prospero expresses his disappointment and loss when he says, "that a brother should/ Be so perfidious! – he whom next thyself/ Of all the world I loved."

The natural hierarchy, often referred to as degree, had been a major theme throughout Shakespeare's great tragedies. In *Troilus and Cressida,* Ulysses warns about the dire consequences of breaking the natural law (Act I, Scene 3). "Take but degree away, untune that string/ And hark what discord follows." We see this discord immediately in the evil nature of Prospero's expulsion from his dukedom in Milan. The sinister and hurried act of putting him and his three-year-old daughter out to sea to drown was committed at midnight "i' th' dead of darkness." Further discord that is a direct result of the overthrow of Prospero's dukedom is gradually revealed as the play progresses.

The magic of Prospero is an all-pervasive dramatic element of *The Tempest.* Its success with the audiences of Shakespeare's day

depended to some degree upon their belief in magic. Dryden's "Prologue to *The Tempest*," written in 1667, sheds some light on
Shakespeare's use of magic in relation to his audience.

> But Shakespeare's magic could not copied be;
> Within that circle none durst walk but he.
> I must confess 'twas bold, nor would you now
> That liberty to vulgar wits allow,
> Which works by magic supernatural things;
> But Shakespeare's power is sacred as a king's.
> Those legends from old priesthood were received,
> And he then writ, as people then believed.
> > Dryden/ Davenant "Prologue to *The Tempest*," 1354-55

Dryden is implying that theater audiences of Shakespeare's day
believed in magic. By Dryden's time people had developed a skep-
ticism about magic. Consequently, Dryden and Davenant collabo-
rated in adapting *The Tempest* for audiences of their own time.

Parliament's statute against the practice of witchcraft and the
conjuration of evil spirits was enacted in 1563 under Queen Elizabeth and confirmed again in 1604 under the rule of James I. It has
been noted by commentators that in the light of these sixteenth
and early seventeenth-century laws, Shakespeare was careful to
make a distinction between the "white magic" of Prospero and the
"black magic" of Sycorax, an evil witch who had ruled the island
before Prospero's arrival. It was believed that she relied on the devil
for her magical powers. Some critics feel that Prospero used his
magic to protect the good characters and punish the evil ones;
hence the name, white magic.

In Prospero's long discourse on the loss of his dukedom and
his subsequent arrival on the island, he frequently addresses
Miranda with questions like "Dost thou attend me?" to make sure
she is still listening. Her short and insignificant responses are a
dramatic device, changing Prospero's monologue into a dialogue
appropriate for the stage.

Study Questions

1. Why does Miranda ask her father to calm the storm at sea?

2. How does Prospero comfort Miranda's fears about the suffering people on the ship?

3. Does Miranda remember anything about her life before she came to the island?

4. How old was Miranda when they arrived on the island?

5. In what way did Antonio dispose of Prospero and Miranda after he had usurped his dukedom?

6. Why did Antonio spare the lives of Prospero and Miranda?

7. Why did Antonio put Prospero and Miranda on an old boat without a sail?

8. Where did Prospero and Miranda get their supplies for the island?

9. Why did Prospero raise the storm at sea with his magic?

10. How long had Prospero and Miranda lived on the island?

Answers

1. Miranda knows that he has raised the tempest with his magic and he also has the power to calm the storm.

2. Prospero tells Miranda that there has been "no harm done."

3. Miranda remembers that several women waited on her in Milan.

4. Miranda was not yet three when they arrived on the island.

5. Prospero and Miranda were put on a "rotten carcass of a butt" without a sail and left on the sea to drown.

6. Prospero was well loved by his people and Antonio wanted to stay in their good graces as the new Duke of Milan.

7. Antonio wanted their deaths to look like an accident.

8. Gonzalo, the king's councilor, felt sorry for them, stocking their leaky vessel with water, food, clothing, and Prospero's books.

9. It had been his good fortune to have his enemies arrive off the shore of the island, and this was his chance to regain his dukedom.

10. Prospero and Miranda had lived on the island for the past 12 years.

Suggested Essay Topics

1. A primitive island and a civilized Milan are the two opposing worlds of the play. Compare these two worlds in view of the theme of illusion versus reality. In what way is the island an illusory world? In what way is Milan the world of reality? Do the leaders of Milan harbor any illusions? Give examples from the play to support your opinion.

2. The people of Shakespeare's day believed that the natural order was based on the hierarchy of all beings. In what way does this idea apply to the usurpation of Prospero's dukedom? What was the result when Antonio became the new Duke of Milan? How did his actions affect the natural harmony of Milan? How did it affect the mutual trust between the two brothers? Cite examples from the play to explain your answer.

Act I, Scene 2, lines 189-320

New Character:

Ariel: *an airy spirit under Prospero's servitude who performs acts of magic for him*

Summary

Prospero calls forth his spirit, Ariel, who appears, reporting that he has created the tempest just as he was instructed to do. Moreover, he has created quite a spectacle on board ship. He has caused the lightning and thunder claps while the mighty sea roared and the "bold waves trembled." Prospero praises him for maintaining his composure in spite of the uproar. Ariel continues, telling him that all except the mariners plunged into the foaming sea in fear and desperation. They have all landed, safe and unblemished, on the shore. He has dispersed them in troops around the island, but left Ferdinand, the king's son, by himself. The king's ship has been stowed in a deep inlet of the harbor with the mariners sleeping under the hatches. The passengers on the other ships of the fleet, thinking the king is dead, are on their way back to Naples.

Prospero again commends Ariel for an excellent performance but tells him there is still more work to be done. Ariel complains, reminding Prospero of his promise to give him his liberty. Prospero tells him to remember what he has done for him. He has saved Ariel from the "foul witch Sycorax" who had imprisoned him in a "cloven pine." Meanwhile, she died and left him in torment for 12 years. When Prospero arrived on the island, he heard Ariel's painful cries and used his art of magic to release him from the pine.

Though Ariel thanks him, Prospero, nevertheless, threatens to peg him into an oak tree to howl away for 12 more years if he continues to grumble. Apologizing, Ariel promises to follow his master's orders. Prospero rewards him by telling him he will be free in two days. This is good news for Ariel, and he is eager to cooperate. He is then sent to disguise himself as a "nymph o' th' sea" and appear invisible to all except Prospero. Ariel quickly obeys.

While Ariel is gone, Prospero awakens Miranda whom he has put into a deep sleep. Together they prepare a visit to Caliban, Prospero's slave. Miranda calls him a villain, but Prospero assures her they could not do without him. He makes their fires, fetches their wood, and does other odd jobs around their cell. Just as he summons Caliban, Ariel appears dressed like a water-nymph. Prospero whispers in Ariel's ear, and he is sent off to do his master's bidding.

Analysis

On the island, Prospero's magic is, in most cases, performed by Ariel. It is Ariel who raises the tempest under Prospero's direction. After the tempest, Ariel's greeting to Prospero appropriately represents the elements of air, water, and fire from which he is derived. As a spirit, Ariel can fly, swim, or "dive into the fire." In ancient times it was believed that the elements of air, water, and fire were the fundamental constituents of the universe. As a spirit of the island, Ariel embodies these elements that emanate from him at various times. He can divide himself and become fire as he does on the king's ship during the course of the tempest.

I flam'd amazement. Sometime I'ld divide
And burn in many places; on the topmast,
The yards and boresprit, would I flame distinctly,
Then meet and join.

Act I, Scene 2, ll. 198-201

Ariel "flam'd amazement" or terrorized the passengers and crew by burning "on the topmast." This alludes to a well-known phenomenon in Shakespeare's day called corposant or St. Elmo's fire, a bluish, luminous glow that would appear on the mast of a ship during an electrical storm at sea. St. Elmo was the patron saint of sailors.

During the storm Ariel mingles with the air, causing Jove's lightning, and with the water, making "Neptune's...bold waves tremble." It is through Ariel's poetic description of the storm that we sense the paradox of this light, airy spirit who was "too delicate/ To act her (Sycorax's) earthy and abhorr'd commands," but could raise a spectacular storm at sea that would strike terror into the passengers and crew.

The magic of the "foul witch Sycorax" is set in stark contrast to the magic of Prospero. In her "unmitigable rage," Sycorax had, with her evil powers, imprisoned Ariel in a "cloven pine" and left him there to groan in agony for 12 years. Prospero, in his benevolence, took pity on him and used his magic to set him free. Sycorax had been banished from Argier (Algiers) because of her "sorceries terrible." It was believed that she relied on devils or evil spirits of the underworld to assist her in these magic acts. Before she died, she had bore a son, Caliban, who was described by Prospero as "a freckled whelp, hag-born," his shape is less than human.

In *The Tempest* Shakespeare observed all three of the Aristotelian unities of action, time, and place. Unity of action requires that the plot must be a unified whole with a beginning, a middle, and an end. Unity of time confined the action to one day only. In this scene Prospero suddenly becomes aware of the time which is "past the mid season./ At least two glasses," or two o'clock in the afternoon. He realizes they must accomplish their work on the island "'twixt six and now." Unity of place limits the action to a single place which is, in the case of *The Tempest*, the island and the sea near the shore. Many of the great playwrights, including Shakespeare (*The Tempest* being an exception), violate at least some of the unities. Modern dramatists put little stress on the importance of the traditional unities but emphasize instead, the single emotional effect of the action.

Study Questions

1. What three elements of nature does Ariel represent in this scene?
2. How does Ariel "burn in many places" during the tempest?
3. What did the passengers of the ship do when they were afraid of dying?
4. What did Ariel do with the passengers?
5. What did Ariel do with the mariners?
6. Where did he leave the ship? Was it damaged from the storm?
7. What does Ariel expect to get for all of his labors?
8. Why is Prospero angry at Ariel for requesting his freedom?
9. Where did the "foul witch Sycorax" imprison Ariel?
10. Why was Ariel left imprisoned for 12 years?

Answers

1. Ariel represents the elements of air, water, and fire.
2. Ariel divides himself and becomes several fires on the ship during the tempest.
3. All except the mariners plunged into the foaming sea.
4. Ariel brought the passengers to the shore, safe and unblemished, and dispersed them in groups around the island.
5. Ariel put them to sleep and left them in the ship.
6. Ariel left the ship in a deep inlet of the island. The ship was undamaged from the storm.
7. Ariel expects Prospero to give him his liberty in exchange for his services.

8. Prospero reminds Ariel of the time he saved him from the curse of Sycorax, and now he feels that Ariel owes him his services.

9. Sycorax imprisoned Ariel in a "cloven pine."

10. Ariel was left in the "cloven pine" because the old witch, Sycorax, had died in the meantime.

Suggested Essay Topics

1. Prospero's magic is set in contrast to that of the "foul witch Sycorax" in this scene. Compare and contrast the magic of Prospero to the magic of Sycorax. In what way could Prospero's use of the supernatural be labelled "white magic"? Was Sycorax practicing "black magic"? How do they compare? How are they different? Cite examples from the play to support your answer.

2. Ariel frightened the passengers as he "flam'd amazement" during the storm at sea. Explicate this term in the light of Ariel's powers as a spirit. In what way does he appear as the element of fire on the topmast of the ship? As the element of air? As the element of water? Would this have been a believable phenomenon in Shakespeare's day? To support your explanation, use examples from the play.

Act I, Scene 2, lines 321-374

New Character:

Caliban: *a deformed, subhuman monster; born from the union of the evil witch Sycorax and a devil*

Summary

With harsh and abusive language, Prospero rudely calls for Caliban, his slave. Caliban, in turn, curses his master and Miranda for subjecting him to the hard labor of carrying logs. Prospero threatens to punish Caliban for his show of disrespect by having urchins or goblins in the form of hedgehogs trouble him all night long with their painful pinches.

Caliban retaliates further by declaring that the island really belongs to him since he has inherited it from his mother, Sycorax. Before Prospero took it from him, Caliban was his own king, but now he has been relegated to the position of Prospero's only subject on the island. Reminiscing about better days, Caliban remembers the time when Prospero and Miranda had just arrived on the island. Prospero treated him with kindness then, giving him food to eat and teaching him the names of the sun and moon. Out of love for Prospero, Caliban had shown him where to find fresh water and land fertile enough to grow food. He regrets his former show of kindness because he is now forced to stay imprisoned in a rock and engage in hard labor for Prospero. He curses himself for what he has done, calling upon the magic of Sycorax to bombard Prospero with toads, beetles, and bats.

Prospero is furious, calling him a "lying slave" who can only be made to understand with harsh beatings rather than with kindness. Prospero reminds Caliban of the care he has bestowed on him, lodging him in his own cell until his attempted rape of Miranda, his own daughter. Showing no remorse, Caliban only wishes Prospero would not have prevented him from populating the island with Calibans.

Miranda chastises Caliban for being capable of doing only evil. When he was an ignorant savage, she took pity on him, teaching him to speak her language. Though he was able to learn, it was his "vild race" that made it impossible for good people to tolerate his presence. Caliban rebukes Miranda, hoping the "red-plague" will destroy her as a retribution for teaching him language. His only benefit has been that he now knows "how to curse." Prospero warns Caliban not to neglect his duties, or he will be given such severe cramps and aching bones that his cries of pain will frighten the beasts. In an aside, Caliban finally decides to obey, realizing the power of Prospero's magic which would control even his mother's god, Setebos.

Analysis

When Prospero summons Caliban from the rock where he is imprisoned, he refers to him as earth. "What ho! slave! Caliban!/ Thou earth, thou! speak (Act I, Scene 2, l. 314). Just as Ariel embodies the elements of air, water, and fire, which was reviewed elsewhere in the text, Caliban represents the element of earth. The spirituality of Ariel is seen in contrast to the earthiness of Caliban. He was the son of the witch, Sycorax, whose "earthy and abhorr'd commands" (Act I, Scene 2, l. 273) were too much to bear for Ariel, a delicate spirit.

It is generally agreed by critics that the character of Caliban is based on the primitive savage of the New World. For *The Tempest*, Shakespeare used Montaigne's essay "Of the Canniballes" which examines the life of the cannibal inhabitants of what would be present-day Brazil. Montaigne describes the lives of the savages as uncorrupted and natural in contrast to those of the corrupt and civilized Europeans. In the case of Caliban, Shakespeare would have it the other way around. Caliban is portrayed as a subhuman monster "got by the devil himself" (Act I, Scene 2, l. 319). He has tried to violate the honor of Prospero's daughter, and although he has been taught their language, all he has learned is "how to curse."

In the *"Riverside Shakespeare's Names of the Actors"* Caliban is described as "a savage and deformed slave." Caliban is an anagram of "cannibal" which is a derivative of "Carib," a savage race of the West Indies or the New World. Caliban's deformity is described later in the play when he is first seen by Trinculo who wonders what kind of monster he has run across on the island. He is "legg'd like a man; and his fins like arms" (Act II, Scene 2, ll. 33-34). Bewildered, Trinculo thinks he is some "strange fish." This is reminiscent of another reference to a fish-like monster in Shakespeare's *Troilus and Cressida*. It is what Ajax is called when he mistakes the deformed and scurrilous Thersites for Agamemnon, the general. "He's (Ajax) grown a very land-fish, languageless, a monster" (Act III, Scene 3, l. 263).

It was not uncommon to hear stories about deformed, fish-like monsters inhabiting the territories of the New World in Shakespeare's day. Monsters too occupied a "position in the moral scale, below man, just as the angels were above him...they are the link between...the settled and the wild, the moral and the unmoral" (cited by L. Edwards in "The Historical and Legendary Background of the Wodehouse and Peacock Feast Motif in the Walsokne and Braunche Brasses." *Monumental Brass Society Transactions*, VIII.

Pt. vii, 300-11. This quotation raken from Kermode's "Introduction to the *Arden Shakespeare*, p XXXIX). Explorers were coming back from their travels with stories of savage, beast-like creatures with no language, living in the forests without the benefit of the civilizing influences. By the late seventeenth and early eighteenth centuries, even before the days of Darwin, the issues of these savage races as the "missing link" were being raised among the general public.

The tension between the two worlds of the play centers around the issue of natural man versus civilized man. Caliban represents nature without the benefit of nurture (Act IV, Scene 1, i. 188). When Caliban attempts to violate Miranda's honor, he cannot do otherwise because he is a natural man without the benefit of societal restraints. To Miranda, a civilized woman, Caliban is "a thing most brutish" who is "capable of all ill."

In this scene we are introduced to the subplot of the play which is not immediately obvious. In subsequent scenes we will see Caliban's conspiracy to murder Prospero and repossess the island. Caliban voices his rightful claim when he says, "This island's mine by Sycorax, my mother." Ironically, Prospero usurped Caliban's position as king of the island just as Antonio usurped his brother's dukedom in Milan.

Study Questions

1. Who were the parents of Caliban?

2. What did Prospero do for Caliban when he first came to the island?

3. How did Caliban respond to Prospero's treatment of him?

4. Why does Caliban feel that he owns the island?

5. What happened when Prospero took Caliban into his own lodging?

6. What does Prospero do to punish Caliban for his behavior?

7. How has Caliban benefited from learning a language?

8. How is Caliban described in the "Names of the Actors"?

9. What does Prospero threaten to do to Caliban if he does not obey him?

10. Why does Caliban finally decide to obey Prospero?

Answers

1. Caliban's parents were the witch, Sycorax, and, according to Prospero, the devil himself.

2. Prospero treated Caliban with kindness, teaching him language and lodging him in his own cell.

3. Caliban learned to love Prospero and showed him where to find fresh water and fertile soil.

4. Caliban feels that he has inherited the island from his mother Sycorax.

5. Caliban attempted to rape Prospero's daughter, Miranda, after they took him into their lodging.

6. Prospero imprisons Caliban in a rock, subjects him to hard labor, and prevents him from seeing the rest of the island.

7. Caliban says that now, "I know how to curse."

8. Caliban is described as a "savage and deformed slave."

9. Prospero threatens to give him painful cramps and aching bones.

10. Caliban obeys because Prospero's art of magic has the power to control even his mother's god, Setebos.

Suggested Essay Topics

1. Caliban's brutish nature is set in opposition to the civilized nature of Prospero and Miranda in this scene. Contrast the two natures in relation to the idea of a corrupted society. Does Caliban seem less corrupt because he is a natural man? How has learning a language affected him? Do Prospero and Miranda seem more corrupt because they are civilized? Cite examples from the play to support your answer.

2. Caliban is described as "a savage and deformed slave" in the "Names of the Actors." Write an essay explaining the idea of savagery and deformity. Give a definition of a savage as it

relates to the sixteenth century and explain how Caliban fits that definition. In what way was Caliban deformed? Why was he subhuman? Would his portrayal have been credible to Shakespeare's audience? Give examples from the play to support your answer.

Act I, Scene 2, lines 375–504

New Character:

Ferdinand: *the son of Alonso, the King of Naples; the prince is later betrothed to Miranda*

Summary

Ariel, invisible to all except Prospero, appears as a "nymph o' th' sea," playing and singing as he leads Ferdinand, the king's son, onto the shore of the island. Addressing his invisible attendant spirits, Ariel instructs them to hush the "wild waves" into silence as they imitate the dance. He welcomes Ferdinand onto the island of domestic habitation with its sounds of dogs and roosters in the distance and the graces of music and harmony to soothe his troubled spirit. The music seems like a supernatural presence to Ferdinand who is unable to locate its source. Drawing him out of the water, the song has had a soothing influence on him, allaying both the fury of the tempest and his grief over his drowned father.

For a while the music stops, but then it begins again. This time in "Full Fadom Five thy Father Lies," Ariel, still invisible, addresses Ferdinand directly to confirm his fears that his father has drowned. He is lying at the bottom of the sea where each part of his body, otherwise doomed to decay, is being transformed into a rich sea substance. Ferdinand is convinced that the music that honors the memory of his drowned father must have some ethereal quality.

As Ferdinand appears on the island, Miranda perceives him as a spirit, but Prospero informs her that he is human. He has survived the tempest, but, although he has a pleasing appearance, he has been misshapen with grief for his lost friends. Still not convinced, Miranda feels he must be a divine being. When Ferdinand first meets Miranda, he is sure she is the goddess who has been singing the songs that led him to the shore. Ferdinand questions Miranda, and she affirms that she is, indeed, human. Prospero promises Ariel his freedom within two days for working his magic on the young couple. Ferdinand then tells Prospero and Miranda that his father, the King of Naples, and all his lords, including the Duke of Milan and his son, disappeared during the storm at sea. He thinks they have drowned since he personally saw their perilous struggle in the raging storm.

In another aside Prospero again addresses Ariel, telling him how pleased he is that, with the help of his magic, the young couple has fallen in love at first sight. For this, Ariel will be rewarded. All is going according to Prospero's plan, but he decides to break off the speedy development of their romantic love to prevent Ferdinand from feeling that Miranda is too easily won. Carrying out a devious plan, Prospero decides to accuse Ferdinand of coming as a spy in order to snatch the lordship of the island from him. Ferdinand denies the charge and Miranda defends him. Prospero quickly censures her for standing up for a traitor. Ferdinand draws his sword, but Prospero uses his magic to freeze his movements. Miranda repeatedly pleads in Ferdinand's behalf, but her father silences her for being "an advocate for an imposter." He tells her it is because of her inexperience that she does not realize there are many men better than Ferdinand. The young prince resolves to endure, in spite of all that has happened to him, if only once a day he will be allowed to see Miranda from his prison. Leading Ferdinand away, Prospero addresses Ariel with words of praise and further plans for still more work to be done.

Analysis

The two songs, "Come unto These Yellow Sands" and "Full Fadom Five thy Father Lies" are set in juxtaposition to enhance their dramatic unity within the context of the play. Both songs assist the dramatic action of the play by ushering Ferdinand onto the shore of the island for the first time and by simultaneously calming the tempest at sea and Ferdinand's grief over his supposedly drowned father.

The mesmerizing power of music in *The Tempest* is analogous to that of the Orpheus myth in Ovid's *Metamorphoses*. Just as "Orpheus sang; and drew wild beasts along,/And rocks and trees, submissive to his song"(Book II, II. 1-2), Ariel's singing and playing leads Ferdinand onto the island. In both cases music has the power to draw or lead its subjects, whether they be beasts or humans, to a desired place. Shakespeare's audiences were familiar with the Orpheus myth and would have easily understood the dramatic function of the music in this part of the play.

Ariel's literal invitation to the dance, eventually leading Ferdinand to Miranda, has symbolic overtones. He will take her hands and together they will kiss "the wild waves whist" or, in other words, still the tempest of the play which represents the hatreds and political rivalries of the past. Their union will bring the opposing sides together and, thereby, offer a peaceful solution to their former conflicts. Symbolically, Ferdinand is being invited to the dance of life which is the fulfillment of love, marriage, and fruition.

Aesthetically the songs function in the dramatic context as lyric poems set apart, by the language, meter, and rhyme scheme, from the blank verse of the rest of the poetic drama. The elements of poetry are evident in the alliteration of "wild waves whist, Foot it featly, sweet sprites, strain of strutting chanticleer," and in the onomatopoeic effects of "Bow-wow" and "Cock-a-diddle-dow." To the song's sense of sound is added the cheerful color of the "yellow sands" and the rhythm of the dance performed by the spirits. "Burthen" indicates the bass to be sung by the spirits but also dispersed by the barking of dogs coming from all corners of the island with chanticleer, the rooster, added to the sound effects of the pastoral scene.

Ferdinand refers to the song as a "sweet air." "Ayre" or "air" was a word used for song in Shakespeare's day, but the word originated with the ancient Greeks. In their operas, the Italians have substituted the word "aria" for "air" in reference to the solos, but etymologically aria came from the word air.

In "Full Fadom Five thy Father Lies" Ariel's song creates the illusion that Ferdinand's father has drowned. This illusory scene is filled with spirits singing and dancing and Prospero's magic controlling the actions of many of the characters. Ferdinand would

have us believe it is "no mortal business." Even Miranda engages in the illusion when she sees Ferdinand's "brave form" and thinks he must be a spirit. As if in a trance, she hardly hears Prospero's explanation but goes on to say, "I might call him/A thing divine, for nothing natural/ I ever saw so noble." For Prospero, who knows the truth, however, the illusory world he is creating with his magic is merely practical reality. Commentators have observed that Prospero has separated Ferdinand from his father on the island so that he can bring Ferdinand and Miranda together, and, thereby, accomplish his purpose which is to restore his dukedom through the marriage of his daughter to Alonso's son.

Further analysis of the aesthetically beautiful lyrics in "Full Fadom Five thy Father Lies" reveals an imagery that substitutes coral for bones and pearls for eyes, lending detachment and perspective to Alonso's supposedly recent death and, in this way, reducing Ferdinand's pain. The heavy alliteration of "Full Fadom Five thy Father Lies" is not picked up again until the fifth line of the song with "suffer a sea-change." The image of Alonso's sea-change, with its beautiful pearl and coral, is symbolic of the change Alonso goes through on the island and reflects the central theme of the play which is repentance, forgiveness, and reconciliation. Alonso's supposed loss of his son in the storm leads him to an acknowledgement of his guilt. By the end of the play Alonso's suffering has changed him. He asks Prospero for forgiveness and restores his dukedom.

Some of the songs can still be sung just as they were written for Shakespeare's audiences. Robert Johnson's setting of "Full Fadom Five thy Father Lies," and "Where the Bee Sucks," appearing later in the play, are both extant settings that were found in John Wilson's *Cheerful Ayres* published in 1660. The original music for "Come Unto These Yellow Sands" has not survived but Long has set it to the music of *The Frog Galliard* by John Dowland, written in 1610. (Both songs can be found in *Shakespeare's Use of Music* by John H. Long. University of Florida Press, Gainesville, 1961.) It is believed that Robert Johnson wrote all the original music for *The Tempest* which has more songs than any other Shakespearean play.

Study Questions

1. Who sings the two songs in this part of the play?

2. Who helps Ariel with the dance in "Come Unto These Yellow Sands"?

3. From where does Ferdinand think the music is coming from?

4. According to the song, what has happened to Ferdinand's father?

5. What is Miranda's first impression of Ferdinand?

6. What is Ferdinand's first impression of Miranda?

7. What is Prospero's false accusation of Ferdinand?

8. Why does Prospero accuse Ferdinand falsely?

9. What is Alonso's sea-change?

10. Name one way in which music assists the dramatic action of the play?

Answers

1. Ariel sings the songs in this part of the play.

2. Ariel's invisible attendant spirits help him with the dance.

3. Ferdinand thinks the music comes from some god of the island.

4. Ferdinand's father has supposedly drowned and now "suffers a sea-change."

5. Miranda thinks Ferdinand is a spirit when she first sees him.

6. Ferdinand thinks Miranda is the goddess who has led him onto the shore with her music.

7. Prospero accuses Ferdinand of coming to the island as a spy so that he could become lord of the island.

8. Prospero falsely accuses Ferdinand because he wants to slow the fast progress of the romantic love between the young couple.

9. Alonso's body is supposedly lying at the bottom of the sea

where each part of it is transformed into a rich sea substance.

10. Music assists the dramatic action of the play by leading Ferdinand onto the island.

Suggested Essay Topics

1. Ariel informs Ferdinand that his father "suffers a sea-change" at the bottom of the sea. Explicate this passage in the light of Alonso's crimes while he was still in Milan. How does the "sea-change" symbolize what will happen to him on the island? How will the "sea-change" affect Prospero? How will it affect the world of Milan? Cite examples from the play to support your essay.

2. Ariel invites his invisible attendant spirits to the dance. Write an essay explaining how the dance symbolizes the relationship of Ferdinand and Miranda. How will the young couple imitate the dance in their daily lives? How will their lives affect the kingdom of Milan? To support your view, give examples from the play.

Act II

Act II, Scene 1, lines 1-184

New Characters:

Adrian and Francisco: *lords who accompany Alonso's royal party*

Summary

The scene is set on another part of the island, some distance from Prospero's cell, where Alonso is grieving the supposed loss of his son, Ferdinand. Gonzalo attempts to offer words of comfort by pointing out that losing someone at sea is a common occurrence. It is a miracle that they have survived, considering the odds against them, and he advises Alonso to weigh that comforting thought against his sorrow. In a mood of pensive reflection, Alonso is unable to receive comfort and quietly pleads to be left alone. Insensitive to Alonso's grief, Sebastian and Antonio begin baiting the king about his inability to engage in conversation and even go so far as to make a wager about who will break the silence, Alonso or Adrian. When Adrian speaks, Sebastian bursts out in raucous laughter for having won the wager. Adrian continues, commenting about the sweetness of the air on the island, but Sebastian and Antonio only jeer, muttering about the "rotten" air that is "perfumed by a fen." Conversely, Gonzalo observes the lush, green grass on the island where everything is advantageous to life, but Sebastian tells him he has completely missed the truth.

Gonzalo then points out an unusual phenomenon. Though

their clothes have been drenched in the storm at sea, they look as fresh and new as they did the day they put them on in Africa for the wedding of the king's daughter, Claribel, to the King of Tunis.

The conversation shifts to the marriage of Alonso's daughter. Gonzalo swears there has not been such a queen in Tunis since "Widow Dido's" time. Sebastian brusquely refutes his use of the term "Widow Dido" for Aeneas' lover, and Adrian, sure that the Widow Dido lived in Carthage instead of Tunis, questions Gonzalo's error. In a humorous exchange Sebastian and Antonio ridicule Gonzalo's preposterous claim that Tunis is, indeed, Carthage. "This Tunis, sir, was Carthage."

Alonso suddenly becomes extremely annoyed at their conversation and regrets giving consent for his daughter's marriage in Tunis which has resulted in the death of his son. Afraid he might never see his daughter again, since Tunis is so far from Italy, he grieves the loss of both a son and a daughter. Francisco tries to comfort the king, assuring him that he saw Ferdinand swimming to shore with "lusty strokes" during the tempest and feels that he must still be alive. Alonso immediately responds with the certainty that his son is gone.

Sebastian tells Alonso he has himself to blame for the loss of Ferdinand. If only he had not given his daughter in marriage to an African instead of a European, Ferdinand would still be alive. Sebastian claims that her unwillingness to marry outside of her country was outweighed by her obedience to her father. Gonzalo reprimands Sebastian for being insensitive at a time like this.

Gonzalo then ruminates about the island, expressing his dream of the ideal commonwealth. He would keep the island in its natural state where everyone would be equal with no riches or poverty. He would govern so perfectly that the time would "excel the golden age." Alonso stops Gonzalo, since his talk means nothing to him. Gonzalo tells the king he was only entertaining the other gentlemen, giving them occasion to laugh at nothing like they always do. When they tell him they were laughing at him, he replies that he is nothing to them so, therefore, they were still laughing at nothing.

Analysis

At the opening of the play, we first meet Sebastian and Antonio during the storm at sea. They find themselves at odds with the Boatswain, cursing him for not doing what they consider a proper job. Sebastian calls him a "bawling, blasphemous, incharitable dog", and Antonio follows these expletives with "you whoreson, insolent noisemaker!' (Act I, Scene 1, lines 40-44). They have met their match in the Boatswain, however, who has no time for the social graces, nor does he care about social position during the storm as he rudely orders them out of his way. The characterization of Sebastian and Antonio in Act II is consistent with our first impressions of them. They are generally insensitive, cynical, and destructive. Gonzalo's attempts to comfort Alonso in his grief for his lost son are immediately thwarted with the sarcastic jeering of Sebastian and Antonio. The coarseness of both of their natures comes into bold relief when their speeches concerning the island are set in juxtaposition to those of Adrian and Gonzalo.

Adrian:	The air breathes upon us here most sweetly.
Sebastian:	As if it had lungs, and rotten ones.
Antonio:	Or, as 'twere perfum'd by a fen.
Gonzalo:	Here is every thing advantageous to life...How lush and lusty the grass looks! How green!
Antonio:	The ground indeed is tawny.

Though he is generally insignificant to the action of the play, Adrian represents the true courtly gentleman who functions primarily as a foil to Sebastian and Antonio in this scene.

Alonso's grief for Ferdinand overwhelms him and brings with it feelings of guilt which will eventually lead him to repentance, forgiveness, and regeneration by the end of the play. For Sebastian and Antonio, who cannot even feel sympathy for a grieving father nor any remorse for their actions, forgiveness and reconciliation will be out of reach.

Gonzalo's speech in which he expounds on his idea of the ideal commonwealth alludes heavily to Montaigne's essay "Of the Canniballes" which has been discussed elsewhere in the text. In idealizing the natural society, untouched by the civilized European, Montaigne describes "A nation...that hath no kinde of traffike, no knowledge of Letters, no intelligence of numbers, no name of magistrate, nor of politike superioritie; no use of service, of riches or of povertie; no contracts, no successions, no partitions, no occupation but idle; no respect of kindred, but common, no apparell but naturall, no manuring of lands, no use of wine, corne, or mettle...How dissonant would hee finde his imaginarie commonwealth from this perfection?" (Montaigne, "Of the Canniballes" translated by John Florio, 1603. This extract taken from Kermode's "Introduction to the *Arden Shakespeare, The Tempest.*"Appendix C 146)

Montaigne's idea of a natural society versus a civilized society dates back to the time of Plato. It was of particular significance to the sixteenth century, however, in the light of the New World discoveries. European explorers were constantly encountering people living in a primeval state of nature without the benefit of civilization as the Europeans knew it. The attractive simplicity of the lifestyle drew many followers who idealized the natural society and the natural man. The myth of the "noble savage" grew out of these beginnings. In *The Tempest* Shakespeare addressed the contemporary issues of Montaigne's ideal society. Compare Gonzalo's speech in this scene to Montaigne's essay on the ideal commonwealth.

> I' th' commonwealth I would, by contraries,
> Execute all things; for no kind of traffic
> Would I admit; no name of magistrate;
> Letters should not be known; riches, poverty,
> And use of service, none; contract, succession,
> Bourn, bound of land, tilth, vineyard, none;
> No use of metal, corn, or wine, or oil;
> No occupation, all men idle, all;
> And women too, but innocent and pure;
> No sovereignty-

Though the similarity to Montaigne's commonwealth is readily apparent, the irony is clear. Gonzalo would still be the king. It is Antonio who points out that "The latter end of his commonwealth forgets the beginning." At the end of his speech, Gonzalo would have "no sovereignty" but at the beginning he says he would be the king who establishes the ideal commonwealth.

Gonzalo's reference to "Widow Dido" alludes to Virgil's *The Aeneid* in which Aeneas sails from Carthage to Cumae just as Alonso and his royal court have sailed from Naples to Tunis. Aeneas, a widower, falls in love with Dido, who is a widow, when he arrives at Carthage. She later commits suicide when Aeneas deserts her. Antonio reacts violently to Gonzalo's term "Widow Dido" probably because she was, in fact, Aeneas' lover, not his wife. Antonio is ridiculing Gonzalo's propriety in referring to her as a widow rather than a lover.

Study Questions

1. Why is Alonso feeling depressed and sad?

2. How do Antonio and Sebastian react to Alonso's depressed mood?

3. How does Adrian feel about the atmosphere of the island?

4. What is Adrian's main dramatic purpose in this scene?

5. What happened to the garments of the royal party during the storm at sea?

6. Who was "Widow Dido"?

7. Why does Alonso feel that he suffers a double loss?

8. Why does Sebastian tell Alonso he has himself to blame for his son's death?

9. Who would manage Gonzalo's ideal commonwealth?

10. How does Alonso feel about Gonzalo's proposed commonwealth?

Answers

1. Alonso is grieving the supposed loss of his son Ferdinand.

2. Sebastian and Antonio are rude and insensitive to Alonso.

3. Adrian feels that the island is uninhabitable, yet the air is sweet and the climate is temperate.

4. Adrian acts as a foil to Antonio and Sebastian who are cynical and abusive.

5. Their garments were drenched but now they are as fresh as they were the day they put them on in Africa.

6. "Widow Dido" alludes to Aeneas' lover in Virgil's *The Aeneid.*

7. Alonso feels he has lost his daughter in marriage to a man in a distant country and has lost his son in the tempest at sea.

8. Sebastian is implying that Alonso forced his daughter to marry a foreigner. It was their trip to the wedding that caused his son's death.

9. Gonzalo would be the king of the commonwealth.

10. Alonso does not want to hear about Gonzalo's commonwealth.

Suggested Essay Topics

1. Gonzalo's ideal commonwealth is patterned after that of Montaigne. Compare and contrast the two societies. In what way is Montaigne's natural society ideal? How does Gonzalo's commonwealth measure up to that ideal? What is the irony of Gonzalo's so-called primeval society? Are there any elements of European civilization in either of the two societies? Cite examples from the play to support your argument.

2. Sebastian and Antonio demonstrate relentless cruelty to Alonso who is grieving for his son. Write an essay analyzing their hope of receiving forgiveness and reconciliation by the end of the play. Do Sebastian and Antonio feel guilty for anything they have done in the past? Does Antonio feel guilty about his usurpation of Prospero's dukedom? Do either of them feel guilty about their cruelty to Alonso in this scene? To support your argument, give examples from the play.

Act II, Scene 1, lines 185-328

Summary

Sebastian and Antonio are bantering with Gonzalo when Ariel arrives, playing his somber music. The soothing sound quickly

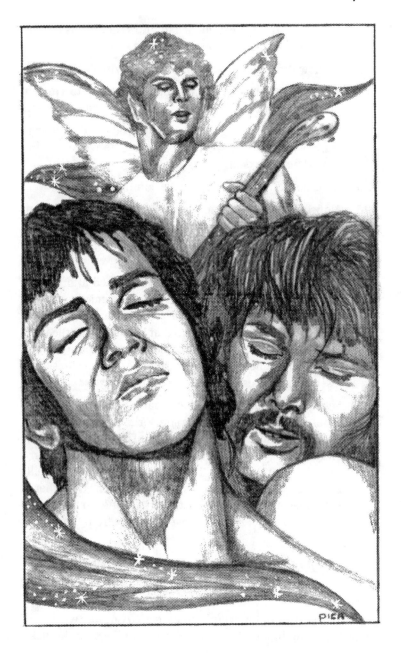

works its magical effects, lulling all except Alonso, Sebastian, and Antonio to sleep. Longing for sleep to shut out his depressing thoughts, Alonso soon feels unusually tired. Antonio assures him that they will stand guard, keeping him safe while he takes his rest.

Sebastian and Antonio are puzzled about the "strange drowsiness" that has suddenly come over the royal party. After the king is asleep, Antonio wastes no time trying to persuade Sebastian that this is his opportunity to replace his brother as king on the throne. With Ferdinand dead and Claribel, his sister, living in the distant land of Tunis, Sebastian is next in line as heir to the throne of Naples. This has not occurred to Sebastian, however, and he is stunned by Antonio's suggestion. Sebastian later admits that, where his political ambition is concerned, he is "standing water." Responding to his metaphor, Antonio tells Sebastian he will teach him "how to flow."

As Sebastian struggles indecisively, he questions Antonio about his conscience regarding the usurpation of his brother's dukedom, but Antonio tells him he feels no guilt. Finally convinced, Sebastian gives Antonio his consent to kill the king. Antonio will draw his sword on Alonso while Sebastian does the same to Gonzalo who would be an obstacle to them if he were allowed to live. The rest of the royal court would obediently follow the new king. Just as they draw their swords, Ariel enters, invisible, to awaken Gonzalo by singing in his ear. Prospero has sent Ariel to stop the conspiracy and save the king's life. Seeing the conspirators with their swords drawn, Gonzalo quickly awakens the king who is shocked at the ghastly sight and asks why they are drawn. Antonio and Sebastian concoct a story about hearing a frightful bellowing that sounded like bulls or lions. Consequently, they drew their swords to protect the sleeping king. Alonso readily accepts their excuse and turns his thoughts to the continuing search for his son. Ariel vows that he will tell Prospero it was his aerial spirit who saved the king's life.

Analysis

In this scene Alonso is finally able to shut out his thoughts about his son's death with the soothing comfort of sleep. Sebastian tells Alonso that sleep "seldom visits sorrow; when it doth,/ it is a comforter." This is reminiscent of an earlier passage in which the visitor is analogous to a minister who would visit a bereaved person. Speaking of Alonso, Sebastian says "He receives comfort like cold porridge" and Antonio responds "The visitor will not give him o'er so" (Act II, Scene 1, lines 10-11). The visitor is the comforter and, in this case, that visitor is sleep. Alonso is finally able to submit to the "heavy offer" of sleep which is his comfort, foreshadowing relief for his sorrow and, ultimately, the healing process of repentance and forgiveness later in the play.

Images of sleep abound in the conversation between Antonio and Sebastian in this scene. When Antonio says that he "sees a crown dropping on thy head," Sebastian wonders whether Antonio is asleep. Antonio points out that if he were asleep, he could not be speaking. Though Sebastian agrees, he argues, nevertheless, that it is a "sleepy language" he is hearing. For Sebastian it is a language that has no purpose and not even a remote possibility. Being the King of Naples has never been his dream. He has simply accepted the fact that Alonso is the king and his children the heirs to the throne. The idea of becoming king is preposterous to Sebastian at first, and he thinks Antonio must be "standing, speaking, moving -/ And yet fast asleep." Antonio responds with yet another sleep image, warning Sebastian that he is letting his fortune or opportunity sleep since he is closing his eyes to it while he is awake.

Critics often compare the character of Antonio to that of Iago in Shakespeare's *Othello*. Antonio will stop at nothing, even the killing of his own brother, to achieve the dukedom of Milan. In comparison, Iago subtly and skillfully plots the destruction of Cassio and Desdemona by falsely accusing them of adultery in order to further his own advancement under the military leadership of Othello. Antonio and Iago can both be described as villains who seek their own ends no matter who pays the price.

When Antonio speaks of the way he has usurped his brother's dukedom, Sebastian reminds him of his conscience. Antonio replies "Ay sir; where lies that?/ ... Twenty consciences/ That stand twixt me and Milan, candied be they,/ And melt ere they molest." Antonio recognizes his guilt, but his conscience is like candy that melts and disappears. Since the usurpation of Prospero's dukedom, Antonio's conscience has been hardened beyond the point of no return. He has lost complete respect for the king's place in the hierarchy. This is strikingly evident in his comment to Sebastian. "Here lies your brother,/ No better than the earth he lies upon." On the issues of kingship, Traversi observes that "once the accepted bonds of conscience and kingship have been broken by an act of usurpation, once the moral foundations of 'degree' have been undermined ... what is to prevent Antonio ... from turning upon the creation of his will. Once he has given his consent Sebastian is as likely as Alonso to be in danger" (Derek Traversi, *Shakespeare: The Last Phase*, 219-20). Whatever the dangers might be, Sebastian decides conclusively to join Antonio in plotting the king's death. Their plot is thwarted, however, when Ariel awakens Gonzalo, singing in his ear, before the conspirators can carry out their evil designs.

Ariel's song seems to be a relatively simple lyric, introduced mainly for its dramatic function which is to incite the characters to act. The song carries a deeper meaning, however, suggesting that as we sleep or are unaware of the evil around us, conspiracy takes over our lives. Drowsiness makes a person vulnerable to conspiracy. In a broader sense, this idea can be applied to Prospero's deposition from his dukedom in Milan. If he would have tended to the business of being a duke, he would have seen that Alonso and Antonio were conspiring against him. Instead, he was wrapped up in his books, unaware of their evil designs.

The imagery of the song suggests a personification of "open-ey'd conspiracy," ready to take Gonzalo's and Alonso's lives unless they "shake off slumber." The alliteration of this line, along with Ariel's admonition to "Awake, awake" are sounds that quickly awaken Gonzalo. Prospero has sent Ariel to awaken the king so that his project, which is the restoration of his dukedom, will not die. The project of restoring Prospero's position as Duke of Milan is, of course, in Alonso's hands and he must, therefore, be kept alive.

Study Questions

1. How does Alonso feel about sleep?

2. What does Antonio do as soon as the king falls asleep?

3. In what way is Sebastian an heir to the throne?

4. How does Sebastian feel when Antonio suggests that Sebastian should be the future king?

5. How does Antonio feel about his conscience?

6. How does Antonio view the king's position in the natural hierarchy or society's law of degree.

7. Who has sent Ariel to stop the conspiracy? Why?

8. What is Prospero's project?

9. Why are Antonio and Sebastian caught with their swords drawn?

10. What was Antonio and Sebastian's excuse for drawing their swords?

Answers

1. Alonso feels that sleep will shut up his thoughts of grief for his son.

2. Antonio tries to persuade Sebastian that Sebastian should replace his brother as the king.

3. With Ferdinand supposedly dead and Claribel, his sister, in Tunis, Sebastian is next in line to the throne.

4. Sebastian thinks that Antonio must be asleep.

5. Antonio's conscience has been hardened beyond the point of no return.

6. Antonio feels that the king is "no better than the earth he lies upon."

7. Prospero has sent Ariel to stop the conspirators so his project will not fail.

8. Prospero's project is the restoration of his dukedom of Milan.

9. Antonio and Sebastian were getting ready to stab Alonso and Gonzalo when Ariel woke them.

10. Antonio and Sebastian claimed they heard the sound of wild animals and drew their swords to protect the king.

Suggested Essay Topics

1. Antonio is often thought of as a villain in *The Tempest.* Write an essay explaining his role as the villain. Is Antonio completely evil? What is his attitude toward his conscience? In what way is he different from Sebastian? Explain his attitude toward power in the play. How far will he go to gain power and position? Cite examples from the play to support your ideas.

2. There are numerous references to sleep in this scene. Write an essay in which you enumerate the sleep images and explicate their meanings. What is Alonso's feeling about sleep and how is it symbolic of his healing process? Explain the meaning of the sleep images used by Antonio and Sebastian. What does Sebastian mean when he says that Antonio speaks a "sleepy language"? Why does Sebastian let his "fortune sleep"? Use examples from the play to support your explanation.

Act II, Scene 2

New Characters:

Trinculo: *the king's jester; companion to Stephano*

Stephano: *the king's drunken butler; Caliban worships him as lord of the island*

Summary

Amidst the noise of thunder, Caliban enters, burdened with wood he is carrying for Prospero, who has enslaved him to his service. Cursing Prospero for the way he is being treated, Caliban delivers a long blustering diatribe describing his torment. When Trinculo enters, Caliban mistakes him for another spirit who has been sent by Prospero to torture him further. Trinculo is wandering around, trying to find shelter from the storm that is brewing when he stumbles onto Caliban. Thinking he has run across a fish-like monster, he decides that someone in England who would ex-

hibit him and charge admission could make a fortune. Just then he hears the rumbling of thunder again and decides to find shelter under Caliban's cloak.

Stephano staggers onto the island in his drunkenness, singing a raucous and bawdy tune. He is happy to be ashore since he has just escaped drowning in the storm at sea and never wants to go to sea again but wishes to live out his life on dry ground. He then discovers Caliban and Trinculo, both sheltered under one cloak, and thinks it is a monster with four legs. Moreover, this strange creature has, somehow, learned his language. If he can "keep him tame," he will take him back to Naples with him and sell him for whatever he can get. Caliban mistakes Stephano for one of Prospero's spirits who has come to torment him. Thinking Caliban is incoherent, Stephano tries to recover him with the wine he has brought ashore. As Caliban drinks, Trinculo's voice is heard under Caliban's cloak. Stephano then decides the monster has four legs and two voices, and he will pour some of the wine into the creature's other mouth. Trinculo calls Stephano's name, and he thinks the monster must be a devil.

Happy to see that Stephano has not drowned, Trinculo emerges from his hiding place under Caliban's cloak and explains that he was trying to escape from the storm. The liquor is now beginning to show its effects on Caliban, and he kneels to Stephano whom he takes for a god bearing "celestial liquor." Stephano and Trinculo exchange stories about their escape. Stephano says he floated ashore on a barrel of wine that had been thrown overboard during the tempest, and Trinculo swears that he swam to shore like a duck.

Caliban, now quite drunk, begs Stephano to be his god, and he will kiss his foot and swear to be his subject. Stephano invites him to do so as Trinculo laughs at a "ridiculous monster" who would "make a wonder of a poor drunkard." Caliban promises to show them the natural wonders of the island, and Stephano tells him to lead the way. Caliban joyously sings his freedom song as he staggers along in the lead. He has found a new master and is finally free of Prospero.

Analysis

As in the case of Ferdinand, our first introduction to Stephano is accompanied by song, but it is a song of a very different nature, revealing the vulgarity of Stephano's character. Critics have commented on the likelihood of Stephano's first song, "I shall no more to sea, to sea," being set to the tune of a funeral song which accounts for Stephano's remark that it is "a scurvy tune to sing at a man's funeral." Shakespeare often alluded to the current popular songs of his day that are unfamiliar to a modern audience.

Stephano has just escaped death by floating to shore on the "butt of sack," which he uses as a comfort from thoughts of his own death. He gives up his attempt at the funeral song and picks up the sea-chantey that he probably learned from the sailors on the ship. Stephano's lusty voice pierces the air with a song about the ship's crew who loved all those women in the song except Kate. She preferred the tailor. The Elizabethans knew well the inferior status of a tailor who is also alluded to in Shakespeare's *King Lear*. Kent, angry with Oswald for his disrespect shown to the king, calls Oswald a cowardly rascal who was made by a tailor. He is certain "a stone-cutter or a painter could not have made him so ill" (*King Lear*, Act II, Scene 2, lines 59-60).

In the first song the heavy alliteration of "shall ... sea, sea/ shall ... ashore" adds to the comic effect. It is heightened further when it reaches "Mall, Meg, and Marian and Margery" which is suggestive of Stephano's view of the sameness of women. "Itch" and "scratch" are tied together in an alliterative bawdy unity. The sensual tone of the song is appropriate to Stephano's character and portrays him as an element of discord on the island.

Permeated with illusory images, this scene is beset with a strange four-legged, two-voiced monster, a god who "bears celestial liquor," and visions of spirits who, in Caliban's imagination, threaten to torment him. When Caliban takes Stephano for a "brave god," he readily accepts this new power which is based on the illusion of a bottle of wine. It is Trinculo who is, perhaps, the most realistic of the three when he sees Caliban as "A most ridiculous monster, to make a wonder/ of a poor drunkard." Together the three of them, with Caliban in the lead, begin their tour of the island which will soon be Stephano's kingdom. Though it is an illusion, it is in the light of his new-found freedom from his service to Prospero that Caliban sings his song.

The song functions dramatically as a turning point for Caliban. Stephano is Caliban's new master, and he will no longer need to work for Prospero who forced him to make dams or weirs for fish, gather wood, scrape trenchers or cut boards for food, and wash dishes. The alliteration is evident in "for fish, fetch in firing, wash dish." The tone of the song is one of abandoned joyousness, expressing Caliban's rebellion against Prospero's oppression. The song is symbolic of freedom, but that freedom is an illusion based on the effects of the "celestial liquor" and a god who is an imposter. Caliban realizes by the end of the play "What a thrice-double ass/ Was I to take this drunkard for a god" (Act V, Scene 1, pages 296-7).

Commentators generally agree that Caliban is superior to Stephano and Trinculo. Caliban's superiority is clearly seen in the poetry of his expression. He usually speaks in the iambic pentameter of Shakespeare's poetic drama, whereas Stephano and Trinculo speak in the mundane prose assigned to the servants or working class in Shakespeare's plays. Even when Caliban curses Prospero for his severe treatment of him, his catalogue of complaints lend full advantage to the beauty of the language.

Though Caliban has found a new master, ironically he will do the same for Stephano and Trinculo as he had done for Prospero 12 years earlier when he showed him "all the qualities o' th' isle,/ The fresh springs, brine-pits, barren place and fertile" (Act I, Scene 2, lines 337-38). Compare the promises he gives to Stephano and Trinculo. "I'll show thee the best springs, I'll pluck thee berries/ I'll fish for thee." He even promises to "get thee wood enough," a service he had detested when he was Prospero's slave.

Study Questions

1. What does Trinculo think he has discovered when he first meets Caliban?

2. Where does Trinculo hide from the impending thunderstorm?

3. How did Stephano arrive at the shore of the island?

4. How did Trinculo get to the shore?

5. What does Stephano think he has found when he runs across

Caliban's cloak with four legs protruding?

6. How does Stephano's wine affect Caliban?

7. What does Caliban ask Stephano to be?

8. What promises does Caliban make to Trinculo and Stephano?

9. What is the central idea in Caliban's song?

10. What does Trinculo think about Caliban's worship of Stephano as his god?

Answers

1. Trinculo thinks he has run across some fish-like monster of the island.

2. Trinculo hides under Caliban's cloak with him.

3. Stephano floated to the shore on a barrel of wine.

4. Trinculo swam to the shore like a duck.

5. Stephano thinks he has found a four-legged, two-voiced monster.

6. Caliban believes Stephano is a "brave god" who "bears celestial liquor."

7. Caliban asks Stephano to be his god.

8. Caliban promises to show Trinculo and Stephano all the natural wonders of the island.

9. Caliban's song expresses a joyous freedom from his master, Prospero.

10. Trinculo thinks Caliban is a "ridiculous monster" who would "make a wonder of a poor drunkard."

Suggested Essay Topics

1. Most critics feel Caliban is superior to Stephano and Trinculo in the play. Write an essay comparing Caliban to Stephano and Trinculo. Compare the language of the three characters. Why does Caliban speak in verse? Why do Trinculo and

Stephano speak in prose? Does Shakespeare consider Caliban superior? To support your argument, choose examples from the play.

2. *The Tempest* contains more songs than any other play in the canon. Write an essay explaining the dramatic function of Stephano's songs in this scene. How do they delineate his character? Why are they both "scurvy" tunes? What is his attitude about women? Cite examples from the play to support your essay.

Act III

Act III, Scene 1

Summary

As the scene opens, Ferdinand is carrying logs under the command of Prospero who has enslaved him with his magic. Though he is forced to stack thousands of logs, "sweet thoughts" of Miranda refresh his labors. Miranda enters, pleading with him to take a rest. Unaware of Prospero's presence, she reasons that her father will be busy with his books for the next three hours, and it would be safe for Ferdinand to sit down for a while. He argues that the sun might set before he finishes his work. In desperation she begs him to relax while she takes over his log-carrying, but he refuses to subject her to such dishonor.

In an aside Prospero speaks of Miranda's romantic love for Ferdinand as if it were an infectious disease. Ferdinand then asks Miranda her name in case he might decide to use it in his prayers. Despite her father's previous warning, she divulges her name to Ferdinand. He goes on to tell her he has known several other women in the past, but each one has had some defect. Miranda is perfect, however, possessing the best virtues of these women all rolled into one. Miranda admits she has known no other women and no men besides Ferdinand and her father. The jewel in her dowry is modesty, and her desire is for Ferdinand alone. He informs her that he is a prince and possibly a king, though he wishes the latter were not true. He tells her that the minute he saw her, his heart became a slave to her services. He assures her that it is for her sake that he bears the burden of carrying logs. She asks him whether he loves her, and he calls out to heaven and earth to hear his declaration of love for her. Overwhelmed with emotion, Miranda begins to cry and immediately chides herself for weeping, because she is happy.

Prospero, still on the sidelines, calls on the heavens to bless the young couple's rare love for each other. Ferdinand asks Miranda why she is crying, and she replies that she is unworthy to offer her love to him and also to expect to receive love in return. Speaking plainly, she asks to become his wife if he would marry her. Whether he marries her or not, she will be his maid or servant until she dies. Reaching out, Ferdinand extends his hand to Miranda and, with a willing heart, agrees to become her husband. She bids him farewell, telling him she will be back in half an hour, and he responds exuberantly with a "thousand" farewells as they both exit.

Left alone, Prospero rejoices at the prospect of his daughter's marriage to the king's son. He hurries back to his studies since there is much to be done before supper.

Analysis

In the opening of this scene, Ferdinand is bearing the burden of carrying logs for Prospero which is comparable to the previous scene where Caliban also carries logs for his master. Both are acting under Prospero's coercive powers, but Ferdinand's reaction to his duties is set in stark contrast to Caliban's. Though his "mean task" would ordinarily be "odious," Ferdinand feels he is bearing logs in the service of his mistress which makes his "labors pleasures." Kermode observes that Ferdinand "quickly understands the purpose of his suffering because he has the power properly to estimate the value of the reward" (Frank Kermode, "Introduction to *The Arden Shakespeare,*" page LVIII). That reward will be Miranda's hand in marriage, and it is this anticipation that gives Ferdinand's log-bearing a special purpose.

Conversely, Caliban sees Prospero's magical powers over him as an instrument of fear. As Caliban increasingly opposes Prospero's designs on him, he is punished with spirit-like apes and hedgehogs that bite and pinch, never giving him any peace. Caliban did, of course, violate the honor of Miranda (Act I, Scene 2, lines 347-48)

and now suffers, according to Miranda, a well-deserved punishment which he brought upon himself by following the uncivilized instincts of his savage nature. By contrast Ferdinand's treatment of Miranda constitutes a polite restraint which is in keeping with his courtly manner. Both are given a soliloquy in the opening of the scene. Caliban's verse, distinctly more poetic than Ferdinand's, shows that he has, indeed, learned how to curse as he has told Miranda earlier in the play.

Characteristic of the romance tradition, Ferdinand and Miranda's love is subjected to great difficulty. Miranda watches anxiously as Ferdinand bears the trial of log-bearing, imposed upon him by Prospero, which is, as we learn later, a trial of love for Miranda. In a subsequent scene Prospero explains to Ferdinand, "All thy vexations/ Were but my trials of thy love, and thou/ Has strangely stood the test" (Act IV, Scene 1, lines 5-7). As is also typical of the romances, Ferdinand's idealized love for Miranda is based on the illusion that she is a pure image of chastity who far outranks any of the other women he has known previously. The hyperbole in Ferdinand's expressions of love for Miranda raises her to the level of the ideal woman. "But you, O you,/ So perfect and so peerless, are created/ Of every creature's best."

When he first meets her, Ferdinand is sure she must be a goddess. Miranda, who has never seen any other men besides Prospero and Caliban, thinks Ferdinand is a divine spirit who has just arrived on the island. It is clearly love at first sight, and he barely knows her name when they decide to marry.

At the close of the scene, Prospero is left on the stage to reflect on the progress of his overall plan which is to restore his dukedom in Milan. It is in his design to marry his daughter to the prince of Naples (Ferdinand) which would be an expedient political move for the former duke since it would join the two royal families. With his magic he has brought Ferdinand and Miranda together on the island and he is now rejoicing because everything is going according to his plan.

Study Questions

1. Why does Ferdinand have a positive attitude about carrying logs?

2. How does Miranda feel about Ferdinand's hard labor of carrying logs?

3. What does Miranda offer to do for Ferdinand?

4. How does Ferdinand respond to Miranda's offer?

5. How does Miranda compare to other women Ferdinand has known?

6. Why does Miranda begin to cry?

7. Why does Ferdinand call himself the king?

8. Who proposes marriage in this scene?

9. What will Miranda do if Ferdinand does not want her for his wife?

10. How does Prospero feel about his daughter's marriage to Ferdinand?

Answers

1. Although it is an "odious" task, Ferdinand feels he is carrying logs for Miranda which makes the job a pleasure.

2. Miranda is anxious about Ferdinand's condition and pleads with him to sit down and rest for a while.

3. Miranda offers to carry Ferdinand's logs for a time.

4. Ferdinand says he would rather break his back than subject Miranda to such dishonor.

5. Miranda represents all the best virtues of all the women rolled into one.

6. Miranda cries because she is so happy.

7. Ferdinand calls himself the king because he thinks his father is dead, and he is next in line as heir to the throne.

8. Miranda asks Ferdinand to marry her, and she will be his wife.

9. Miranda will be Ferdinand's maid or servant if she cannot be his wife.

10.   Prospero has designed the match, and he is happy that ev-
       erything is going according to his plan.

Suggested Essay Topics

1.   Ferdinand carries logs for Prospero at the opening of the
     scene just as Caliban did in the previous scene. Compare and
     contrast Ferdinand's soliloquy in this scene with Caliban's
     in the last scene. In what way are they similar? How are their
     attitudes set in contrast to each other? What are the reasons
     for the difference? Give examples from the play to support
     your view.

2.   In the romantic tradition the lovers are idealized and sub-
     jected to great difficulties during the course of their love.
     Write an essay describing Ferdinand and Miranda's love in
     the light of the romantic tradition. In what way does
     Ferdinand idealize Miranda? Describe Miranda's ideal man.
     What trials do they need to overcome in their love relation-
     ship? To support your essay, give examples from the play.

Act III, Scene 2

Summary

Caliban, Stephano, and Trinculo are now quite drunk, and they
are concerned about what they will do when they run out of wine.
Stephano announces that they will simply "drink water" when the
time comes, but not a minute before. Stephano relishes the attentions from Caliban, his servant-monster, and Trinculo ridicules
both of them, reasoning that if their group represents three out of
the five people on the island, and the intellect of the other two is
as low as theirs, the island government must be on the verge of
collapse. Ignoring Trinculo's remark, Stephano continues to focus
his thoughts on Caliban, proclaiming that, when he becomes king,
he will either appoint the monster as his lieutenant or his stan-
dard-bearer. At this point Caliban is too drunk to walk or even
stand, but he feebly salutes Stephano as his king. Trinculo mocks
Caliban, calling him an "ignorant monster" who tells "monstrous

lies." Responding to Caliban's appeal, Stephano threatens to hang Trinculo on the "next tree" if he engages in mutiny. Declaring that the monster is his subject, Stephano swears that he deserves to be treated with dignity. Caliban thanks Stephano and asks him to listen to his proposal. Stephano agrees, instructing Caliban to kneel.

On his knees Caliban begins by explaining that he serves a tyrant who has cheated him out of the island. Ariel, who is invisible, is heard in the background, mimicking Trinculo's voice with "Thou liest." Caliban angrily asserts that he does not lie, and Stephano threatens to supplant Trinculo's teeth with his fist if he continues to trouble the monster. Trinculo swears he said nothing, and finally Caliban continues with a plea to Stephano to avenge Prospero's injustice. If Stephano will dare to reclaim the island, Caliban will serve him as lord on it. Stephano is willing, but as they plot to kill Prospero, Ariel, still imitating Trinculo's voice, repeatedly interferes with the accusation that Caliban is lying. After several warnings, Stephano finally beats Trinculo and asks him to stand back.

Caliban suggests that they catch Prospero in the afternoon while he is napping and seize his books first. Without his books, Prospero is powerless. After that they can either stab him, beat his skull, or cut his throat. Caliban also informs Stephano that Prospero has a beautiful daughter who would "become thy bed" and give him many children. Stephano immediately decides he will kill Prospero. His daughter and Stephano will then reign as king and queen on the island and Trinculo and Caliban will be viceroys. Shaking Trinculo's hand, Stephano apologizes for beating him. Ariel hurries away to his master with news of the conspiracy.

Within a half hour Prospero will be asleep. Filled with joy at the prospect of his new-found freedom, Caliban asks Stephano to sing the song he had taught him earlier. They sing but Caliban notices it is not the right tune. Ariel then assists them on tabor and pipe or, in other words, drum and flute.

Stephano and Trinculo are afraid of the mysterious presence of the music played by invisible Ariel, a "picture of Nobody," but Caliban tells them not to be afraid. He assures them the island is full of "noises, sounds, and sweet airs" that will not hurt them. The music fades away, but its mesmerizing sound leads them, and they decide to follow it.

Analysis

The subplot of the play has been reviewed elsewhere in the text, but it bears repeating in relation to this scene where we see the beginnings of Caliban's conspiracy to murder Prospero and reclaim the island. Caliban had stated earlier that "This island's mine by Sycorax my mother" (Act I, Scene 2, line 331). Formerly he had been his own king, but now he says he is "subject to a tyrant" who has "cheated me of the island." With the help of Stephano and Trinculo, Caliban is now conspiring to repossess the island. This parallels Prospero's plans to repossess his dukedom in Milan. It is ironic that Prospero usurped Caliban's rightful place on the island just as Antonio usurped his brother Prospero's dukedom.

Much has been said about Caliban's thoughts of violence in this scene which have been checked by Prospero thus far in the play. When they are left unchecked, Caliban's natural instincts prompt him to batter Prospero's skull with a log, "paunch him with a stake,/ Or cut his wezand (windpipe) with a knife." Caliban also demonstrates a more subtle and, consequently, a more deadly violence, however, in his implications about Prospero's daughter. She is considered Prospero's possession to be had for Stephano's pleasure and, as a by-product, to populate his kingdom on the island. Earlier, Caliban attempted to rape Prospero's daughter Miranda. When confronted by Prospero, he showed no remorse for his act of violence but simply responds with "O ho, O ho, would't had been done!/ Thou didst prevent me" (Act I, Scene 2, lines 349-50).

To celebrate their decision to murder Prospero and overthrow his kingdom on the island, Stephano, with Trinculo's help, attempts to sing a catch. An Elizabethan catch was equivalent to a modern round song with each singer alternating the beginning to produce a three-part harmony from a single melody. Stephano and Trinculo cannot get the tune, so Ariel comes to their assistance with tabor and pipe. They are awed by the power of Ariel's harmonious music played by the "picture of Nobody" since Ariel is still invisible. Stephano and Trinculo are afraid of the mysterious power of Ariel's music but Caliban, who has a natural appreciation for all the sounds of the island, reassures them. "Be not afeard, the isle is full of noises,/ Sounds, and sweet airs, that give delight and hurt not." It is significant that Caliban is the one to notice that Stephano and

Trinculo are not getting the tune of the catch. Caliban seems to be more in tune with the natural harmony of the island than Stephano and Trinculo.

There is also a dramatic function in their inability to sing the song. When Ariel assists them with tabor and pipe, they follow the music which eventually leads them to the "filthy-mantled pool" (Act IV, Scene 1, line 182).

"Thought is free" was a proverbial expression in Shakespeare's day with the negative connotation of unfavorable or feigned thought. In this catch it not only applies to Stephano and Trinculo, but also to Caliban whose thoughts of freedom from the servitude of Prospero are illusory and lead him into an association with irresponsible and rebellious characters. Thought is certainly not free for these three and the irony of it is clear. Their plot to murder Prospero not only leads them into the bondage of the "filthy-mantled pool" in a subsequent scene but also into the bondage of their moral, intellectual, and spiritual natures. They are not free at all, but bound to their "butt of sack" which is their only "comfort." The irony goes even further than that, however. The island is now Prospero's kingdom and although thought might be free for a while, the consequences of free thinking only lead to a greater bondage.

Study Questions

1. Why is Caliban unable to walk in the beginning of this scene?

2. What is Caliban's proposal to Stephano and Trinculo?

3. Who does Caliban suggest as king of the island? What position will Caliban hold?

4. What is Ariel's purpose for mimicking Trinculo's voice?

5. Why does Stephano beat Trinculo?

6. What is the first thing the conspirators intend to do when they reach Prospero's cell?

7. Why are Prospero's books important to the conspiracy?

8. Who notices that Stephano and Trinculo cannot get the tune of the catch?

9. Who is afraid of the mysterious music of Ariel's tabor and pipe?

10. How does the music affect the three characters by the end of the scene?

Answers

1. Caliban is too drunk to walk.

2. Caliban suggests that they murder Prospero and take over the island.

3. Caliban suggests that Stephano be the king of the island and Caliban will be his servant.

4. Ariel's purpose for mimicking Trinculo is to set the characters against each other.

5. Stephano thinks Trinculo is mocking Caliban by calling him a liar.

6. The first thing the conspirators will do at Prospero's cell is seize his books.

7. Without his books Prospero has no magical powers.

8. Caliban notices that they are singing the wrong tune.

9. Stephano and Trinculo are afraid of Ariel's music.

10. The music mesmerizes them, and they follow it.

Suggested Essay Topics

1. The conspiracy to kill Prospero and regain the island is often considered to be the subplot of the play. Write an essay comparing this plot to the main plot. In what way are the two conspiracies comparable? Has Prospero usurped Caliban's kingdom on the island? If so, in what way? How do Prospero's actions compare to the actions of his brother Antonio? Was Caliban the rightful king of the island before Prospero's arrival? Cite examples from the play to support your view.

2. Caliban states that "the isle is full of noises, sounds, and sweet airs, that give delight and hurt not." Explicate this passage in the light of Caliban's nature. How does this speech

reflect Caliban's poetic sensibilities to the natural sounds of the island? Is Caliban more sensitive to the natural harmony on the island than Stephano and Trinculo? In what way? Explain your answer with the use of examples from the play.

Act III, Scene 3

Summary

The king and his royal party, still searching for Alonso's son, are completely exhausted. Gonzalo suggests that they sit down to rest since his old aching bones cannot go any farther. Having lost hope that his son is alive, Alonso too has become weary and decides to rest. Antonio and Sebastian quickly catch Alonso's mood of despair and decide to use it to their advantage. In hushed tones they conspire to murder the king that same night when he and Gonzalo, tired and filled with sorrow, will not be as vigilant as usual.

Prospero appears, invisible, to the tune of "solemn and strange music." Several of Ariel's spirits enter with a banquet, and dance around it. They invite the king to partake of the food as they quickly withdraw from the scene. The members of the royal court are filled with amazement, agreeing that this gives credence to the exotic stories that travelers bring back from their journeys to distant lands. Gonzalo declares that people in Naples would never believe him if he told them of these islanders whose manners are gentler and kinder than those of most humans. In an aside Prospero, applauding Gonzalo's opinion, declares that some people in Naples are, in fact, "worse than devils." Alonso is reluctant to eat, but Gonzalo finally convinces him. The king, in turn, invites Antonio to join him. Just as they reach for the food, Ariel, in the guise of a harpy, enters to the sounds of thunder and the flashes of lightning. He covers the table with his wings and the banquet disappears. No longer invisible, Ariel speaks to the "three men of sin," Alonso, Antonio, and Sebastian, indicting them for their crimes against Prospero 12 years ago. In an attempt to defend themselves, Alonso and Sebastian draw their swords, but Ariel uses his magic to weaken their movements which makes their swords too heavy to lift. Ariel rebukes them for supplanting Prospero from Milan and exposing him and his innocent child to the sea. Now the powers have "incens'd the seas" against them and have taken Alonso's son. The king's only escape from further wrath that might fall on his head is repentance for his past deeds.

Ariel vanishes to the sound of thunder and his spirits return, dancing to soft music as they remove the banquet table. Prospero praises Ariel for following his instructions explicitly. All three men are under Prospero's power now, and he will leave them entangled in their fits of madness while he pays another visit to Ferdinand and Miranda. Gonzalo, who has not heard Ariel speak, wonders why the men are staring into space. Still in a stupor, the king imagines that the dreadful thunder had pronounced the name of Prospero. Suddenly realizing that Ferdinand's death is a retribution for the king's sin against the rightful duke of Milan, Alonso leaves, vowing to join his dead son at the bottom of the sea. Sebastian and Antonio hurry off, threatening violence to Ariel and his legions. Gonzalo sends Adrian and Francisco to follow them and prevent them from committing suicide or other acts of violence they may be provoked to do.

Analysis

The banquet, set before the royal party, is brought "with gentle actions of salutations" by Ariel's spirits. It disappears in quite another way, however. With the sound of thunder and flash of lightning, Ariel appears disguised as a harpy, spreading his wings over the table as the banquet vanishes. In Greek mythology the harpies were represented as birds with the faces of women. Virgil imitates the classic Greek myth in *The Aeneid*. In their travels Aeneas and his men, losing their way in a storm at sea, land on the Strophades, the islands of the harpies. Tired and hungry, they slaughter the oxen and goats and begin to eat.

> Then we spread couches on the winding shore
> And fall a-feasting on the dainty meat.
> But suddenly, with awe-inspiring swoop
> The harpies from the mountains are at hand,
> And with loud flappings shake their wings, and snatch
> Our banquet from us.
>
> Virgil, *The Aeneid*, Book III, lines 231-36

Calaeno, the chief harpy, appears on a high rock to tell Aeneas that Jupiter pronounces judgement on them for slaughtering the harpies' oxen and goats. Calaeno imposes hunger upon them as a punishment for their crime which brings about a consciousness of their guilt. The analogy to the "three men of sin" is clear. Alonso, Sebastian, and Antonio must suffer hunger in order to reach a consciousness of their guilt in the supposed murder of Prospero and his daughter twelve years ago. Ariel's speech is a clear indictment of their crime of supplanting Prospero from Milan and exposing him and his innocent daughter to the sea. For this, Alonso has lost his son, and there is no other way to escape his doom, except by repentance and a sinless life thereafter.

The image of the vanishing banquet is also seen by critics as a symbol of the Eucharist where God sends down the Holy Spirit in the form of a dove (rather than a harpy) to bless the communion table. In the case of the "three men of sin" their guilt and sin must be purged by means of repentance before they can partake of the meal or the sacrificial bread and wine; hence the disappearance of the banquet.

In this scene, critics often interpret Ariel's speech as an affirmation of the Christian concept of recognition of sin and guilt followed by repentance or "heart's sorrow," with a sinless or "clear life ensuing." Alonso immediately recognizes his guilt and is filled with remorse. "The thunder ... pronounced /The name of Prosper; it did base my trespass./ Therefore my son i' th' ooze is bedded." Suffering, brought about by the supposed loss of his son, has led Alonso to a recognition of his sin against Prospero for which he takes full responsibility.

Conversely, Antonio feels no guilt and, therefore, he cannot be purified or regenerated. Earlier in the play, he clearly denies that he has a conscience. "If he does, it simply melts like candy before it bothers him" (Act II, Scene 1, lines 275-280). Though Sebastian's conscience troubles him, he is gullible and eventually agrees to do what is expedient, even if he must kill his own brother in order to become king of Naples. After Ariel's indictment of them, Antonio and Sebastian leave the stage ready to fight legions of an unknown enemy.

Images of the sea abound in the play and many of them are

found in this scene. Alonso's "sea-change" in "Full Fadom Five" (Act I, Scene 2) is a symbol of his change throughout the play. His change has already begun with the recognition of his guilt in the crime of Prospero's deposition and the supposed deaths of the former duke and his daughter. Alonso personifies the sea that "mocks" their search for Ferdinand on land. Ariel refers to the "never-surfeited sea" that belched up the "three men of sin," and later he speaks of the powers that "incens'd the seas" against the peace of the royal party. Alonso's image of the sea is seen as the mud at the bottom where "my son i' th' ooze is bedded." In view of the personification of the sea and the fact that it frequently assists the dramatic action, it would seem plausible to list "the sea" as another character in the play.

Study Questions

1. Why does the royal party stop to rest during their search for Ferdinand?

2. What do Sebastian and Antonio plan to do that night?

3. What do Ariel's spirits bring onto the stage?

4. What does Ariel do when he arrives on the stage?

5. Who does Ariel address in his speech?

6. What does Ariel warn them about in his speech?

7. What does Ariel mean by "heart's sorrow"?

8. What is meant when Ariel refers to "a clear life ensuing"?

9. In what condition are the three men when Prospero leaves them?

10. What does Alonso intend to do by the end of this scene?

Answers

1. Gonzalo, the oldest, suffers from exhaustion, and Alonso feels tired and discouraged in his hopeless search for his son.

2. Sebastian and Antonio are conspiring to kill the king and Gonzalo that same night.

3. Ariel's spirits present the royal party with a banquet.

4. Ariel, in the guise of a harpy, covers the table with his wings and the banquet vanishes.

5. Ariel addresses the "three men of sin," Alonso, Sebastian, and Antonio.

6. Ariel warns them that if they do not repent their sins against Prospero, their doom is certain.

7. There "is nothing but heart's sorrow" means there is no other way except repentance.

8. A "clear life" is a sinless life which should follow repentance.

9. Prospero leaves the three men in their fits of madness.

10. Alonso intends to commit suicide by joining his son at the bottom of the sea.

Suggested Essay Topics

1. Ariel's speech is central to the theme of repentance, forgiveness, and reconciliation. Critics have often interpreted Ariel's speech in the light of the Christian tradition. Write an essay explaining the possible Christian influence on Ariel's speech. What must the "three men of sin" do to avoid their doom? What kind of life must they live thereafter? What sins have they committed? Cite examples from Ariel's speech to explain your answer.

2. The disappearance of the banquet is often seen as an allusion to Virgil's *Aeneid*. Compare and contrast the banquet scene in *The Tempest* to the story of the harpies in Virgil's *Aeneid*. What lesson can be learned from both? Why are the characters in both accounts subjected to hunger as punishment for their sins? How are the stories different? Are the sins in both accounts of equal magnitude? Give examples from Virgil's *Aeneid* and Shakespeare's *The Tempest* to support your argument.

Act IV

Act IV, Scene 1, lines 1-163

New Characters:

Iris: *goddess of the rainbow; Juno's messenger*

Ceres: *goddess of agriculture*

Juno: *goddess of the Pantheon; patroness of marriage; wife of Jupiter*

Nymphs and Reapers: *spirits of the dance*

Summary

The scene begins with Ferdinand culminating his trial of log-bearing. Prospero assures him that his austere punishment has simply been a trial of his love for Miranda, and he has "stood the test." As a reward, Prospero presents him with a "rich gift," his daughter Miranda. He tells Ferdinand that he will soon realize she will be everything her father says she is and more. She now belongs to Ferdinand, but Prospero warns him that if he breaks "her virgin-knot" before they have taken their sacred vows of marriage, hate and discord will accompany their union. Ferdinand vows his honor will never give way to lust even under the strongest temptation. Prospero is satisfied, and he turns his attentions to Ariel, instructing him to gather his lesser spirits for the presentation of the betrothal masque in honor of the young couple. Ariel promises to bring them back in the twinkling of an eye.

Prospero again warns Ferdinand that even the "strongest oaths" can be weakened by one's passions, but the young prince assures him he will keep his passions under control. Prospero directs Ariel to bring an extra spirit in case they need one and then hushes everyone to silence as Iris enters to soft background music. As a messenger of Juno, Iris summons Ceres, goddess of the earth's fertility, to celebrate a "contract of true love." Ceres is concerned that Venus and her son Cupid will be present at the masque. She has avoided their company ever since they helped Pluto plot the abduction of Ceres' daughter, Proserpine, who became his queen in the underworld. Iris assures Ceres that Venus and Cupid will not attend the masque. Having failed in her attempt to cast a licentious spell on Ferdinand and Miranda, Venus' chariot is now headed for Paphos.

Juno arrives and, with the help of Ceres, blesses the honored couple with a song. Juno's blessing carries wishes for a long and happy union in the first part of the song, and Ceres follows with the assurance of a fertile life for the betrothed couple. Ferdinand reacts enthusiastically and joyously to the vision and wishes he could live on the island forever. He thinks that Prospero has the power to create a heaven on earth. Prospero again calls for silence so the spirits will not vanish. Continuing the masque, Iris summons the pastoral Nymphs and Reapers to celebrate the love of the betrothed pair with graceful dancing.

In the midst of the dance, Prospero speaks and the spirits vanish with a "strange, hollow, and confused noise." Prospero has dismissed the spirits, suddenly remembering the conspirators' threats against his life. Ferdinand and Miranda are puzzled at Prospero's strange behavior. Aware of Ferdinand's look of dismay, Prospero explains that the festivities have ended, and the spirits have vanished into the air. Prospero asks Ferdinand to bear with him in his infirmity. Instructing Ferdinand and Miranda to retire to his cell, Prospero tells them he will take a short walk to ease his troubled mind.

Analysis

In this scene Ferdinand has endured his trial of log-bearing, and has, in a sense, reached a purification that prepares him for his union with Miranda and the establishment of the new order that their union represents. Although we never really know the true nature of Ferdinand's guilt, it is probable that Prospero holds Ferdinand responsible, at least in part, for his father's crime, the usurpation of Prospero's dukedom. We know, of course, that Prospero is trying to restrain the passion between Ferdinand and Miranda which represents the processes of nature and fertility that he wishes to control, but, whatever the guilt might be, Ferdinand is forced to pay for it. He endures the harsh treatment for the prize, Miranda.

Prospero orders Ariel to perform the masque for the young couple because "they expect it" from him. The masque song functions mainly to lift the action out of the present and into the future "brave new world" (Act V, Scene 1, line 183) which will be built on the love of Ferdinand and Miranda. Their love and marriage represents a hope for order and harmony where there has been chaos and discord due to the hatred and strife of their fathers.

Although the masque existed in medieval times, it grew in popularity at the end of the reign of Elizabeth I and lasted well into the seventeenth century during the reigns of James I and Charles I. The masque in *The Tempest* includes all the traditional elements: instrumental music, vocal music sung by Juno and Ceres, the dialogue of Juno, Ceres, and Iris, and a "graceful dance" by the Reapers and the Nymphs. We can only conjecture about the costuming and stage setting which was, in the case of the court masques, elaborate and expensive. We know that *The Tempest* was performed at court in February 1613 to celebrate the marriage of the daughter of James I, Princess Elizabeth, to Frederick, Count Palatine. Though appropriate to the occasion of their marriage, the masque is specifically relevant to *The Tempest* and was given increased importance in many of Shakespeare's later plays, such as *Cymbeline* and *The Winter's Tale*.

The masque begins with "soft music" lending an air of solemnity to its formal tone. The pastoral imagery throughout the dialogue and song and the costumes of the Nymphs, with their "rye-straw hats" is in keeping with the naturalism of the island. The purpose of the masque, which is to celebrate the betrothal, is set forth in the dialogue of Ceres and Iris. Juno, with Ceres' assistance,

appropriately sings the song in the masque to bless the marriage and honor the children that are to be born from the union. "Earth's increase" is a reference to everything the earth produces and "foison plenty" is the abundant harvest depicted in the pastoral imagery of this ideal, natural world with its full barns and granaries, clusters of grapes on the vine, and plants that are weighted down with heavy fruits or vegetables.

The abstract language of the masque portrays the abundance that the earth will yield, not only to Ferdinand and Miranda, but also, universally, to men and women who will base their lives and actions on love and harmony rather than hatred and dissonance. The song is a universal statement of love, harmony, fruition, peace, and serenity. It is an ideal to be hoped for, but it takes responsible action, a rare commodity in the power-hungry world Ferdinand and Miranda have inherited.

This ideal world is, after all, only a vision and quickly vanishes into thin air. Prospero explains the nature of this fleeting vision to Ferdinand. The illusory vision of this pageant is compared to life in which all of the palaces, temples, and even "the great globe itself" will eventually dissolve. Our lives too will soon end in death. Many commentators have seen Prospero's famous speech as Shakespeare's farewell to the stage and to the Globe Theater.

> Our revels now are ended. These our actors
> (As I foretold you) were all spirits, and
> Are melted into air, into thin air."
> And like the baseless fabric of this vision,
> The cloud-capp'd tow'rs, the gorgeous palaces,
> The solemn temples, the great globe itself,
> Yea, all which it inherit, shall dissolve,
> And like this insubstantial pageant faded
> Leave not a rack behind. We are such stuff
> As dreams are made on; and our little life
> Is rounded with a sleep.

These were prophetic words since Shakespeare died in 1616, only a few years after *The Tempest* was written, and Prospero's speech reflects the influence of the approaching end to his career.

Study Questions

1. Why did Prospero punish Ferdinand by forcing him to carry logs?

2. What was Ferdinand's reward for standing up under the test of log-bearing?

3. What is Prospero's warning to Ferdinand?

4. What does Prospero instruct Ariel to do in this scene?

5. Which characters are given dialogue in the masque?

6. List the characters who sing the masque song?

7. Explain the reason why Ceres does not want Venus to attend the masque?

8. In whose honor is the masque given?

9. Why does the masque suddenly vanish?

10. In what way does Prospero compare life to the masque or the stage?

Answers

1. Prospero's punishment was a trial of Ferdinand's love for Miranda.

2. Prospero rewards Ferdinand with a "rich gift," his daughter Miranda.

3. Prospero warns Ferdinand that he should not break the "virgin-knot" before he and Miranda have recited their marriage vows.

4. Prospero instructs Ariel to summon his spirits and bring on the masque.

5. Iris, Ceres, and Juno speak during the masque.

6. Juno and Ceres sing the masque song.

7. Venus and her son, Cupid, helped Pluto abduct Ceres' daughter Proserpine.

8. The masque is given in honor of Ferdinand and Miranda,

the betrothed couple.

9. The masque vanishes when Prospero remembers that Caliban and his new-found friends are conspiring to kill him.

10. All the material things of life, including life itself, will eventually dissolve.

Suggested Essay Topics

1. The masque is often interpreted as a ceremony celebrating the union that will usher in the new order or the "brave new world." Write an essay explaining the symbolism of that order in the union of Ferdinand and Miranda. How will their marriage affect the political situation in Milan and Naples? How will it affect Prospero's political position? How will their union affect Alonso? Cite examples from the play to support your view.

2. Prospero's famous speech beginning "Our revels now are ended" is often seen as a poetic statement revealing Shakespeare's philosophical view of life. Explicate this speech in which Prospero compares life to the masque. What has happened to the "insubstantial pageant"? In what way does this compare to all the things that people hold dear? Why are people's lives like a dream? Use examples from the play to support your explanation.

Act IV, Scene 1, lines 164-266

Summary

Prospero anxiously summons Ariel, informing him that they must prepare for the coming of Caliban. Ariel then discloses the latest information about the whereabouts of Caliban, Stephano, and Trinculo. With tabor and pipe Ariel had charmed the three conspirators into following him and left them neck deep in the "filthy-mantled pool" beyond the cell. Prospero praises Ariel, instructing him to remain invisible as he gathers the former duke's royal wardrobe to use as bait to catch the would-be murderers.

Ariel leaves promptly. Left alone, Prospero reflects on the pains he has taken to civilize Caliban. He decides it has all been in vain, considering the fact that Caliban is, after all, a "born devil" who cannot be reformed. His body grows uglier with age, and his actions are becoming more malevolent. Prospero is determined to afflict harsh punishment on all three of the conspirators.

Ariel returns with his arms full of Prospero's wearing apparel and hangs it on a lime tree next to the cell. Caliban, Stephano, and Trinculo enter, wet and reeking with odor from the "filthy-mantled pool." Disgruntled and humiliated, Stephano censures Caliban for assuring him that Ariel is a "harmless fairy." He has, in fact, done nothing but mislead them so far. Caliban pleads with them to "speak softly" to keep from waking Prospero. He promises them that the prize that goes with the kingship, which is Miranda, will make it all worthwhile. Trinculo and Stephano, still distracted by the loss of their bottles in the scum-covered pool, refuse to be comforted.

Hushing them to silence, Caliban signals their approach to the cell where Stephano will murder Prospero and take possession of the island forever. Just as Stephano begins to "have bloody thoughts," Trinculo spots the wardrobe on the lime tree, and Stephano too is drawn to the kingly gowns. Caliban tries to divert their attention, warning them that if Prospero awakes, he will punish them with pinches. Nervously, he implores them to murder Prospero first, or they will surely lose their chance. Ignoring his pleas, Stephano and Trinculo pile his arms with the finery and tell him to help them carry it away. Their thievery ends abruptly, however, when Ariel and Prospero, both invisible, turn spirit-like dogs on them, driving the three away from Prospero's cave. Prospero reminds Ariel he will soon be free, but the enemy is at his mercy this very hour, and he still needs Ariel's services for a little while.

Analysis

In this scene Prospero refers to Caliban as "A devil, a born devil." This is reminiscent of Prospero's earlier words when he calls forth his slave who was "got by the devil himself," (Act I, Scene 2, line 319) and whose mother was the wicked witch Sycorax. Prospero and Miranda had attempted to educate and civilize

Caliban, but their humane treatment of him had been fruitless. Being born to evil parents, Caliban's "vild race had that in't which good natures/ Could not abide to be with" (Act I, Scene 2, lines 359-60). Caliban "on whose nature/ Nurture can never stick," had been taught language, but, as he so aptly puts it, his only profit has been that he has learned how to curse. Taking pains to treat him humanely, Prospero has allowed him to live in his cell, but that has only led to Caliban's attempt to violate Miranda's honor for which he is now being punished.

In escaping his servitude under Prospero, Caliban has now enslaved himself to a worse fate, however, by serving a drunken god whom he worships. He has based his new-found freedom on an illusion which disappears as soon as the effect of the liquor wears off. He later admits, "What a thrice-double ass/ Was I to take this drunkard for a god" (Act V, Scene 1, lines 295-96).

At first sight of Prospero's wardrobe, hanging on the lime tree, Trinculo, imagining Stephano in these kingly robes, bursts out with "O King Stephano! O peer! O worthy Stephano! look what a wardrobe here is for thee!" This alludes to a popular ballad in Shakespeare's day which is also found in *Othello*.

> King Stephen was and-a worthy peer,
> His breeches cost him but a crown;
> He held them sixpence all too dear,
> With that he call'd the tailor lown;
> He was a wight of high renown,
> And thou art but of low degree.
>
> *Othello*, Act II, Scene 3, lines 89-94

Stephano's lack of responsible action as the new king on the island can readily be seen in this episode where he is under the illusion that being king is nothing but dressing in expensive kingly robes and ruling over subjects who are willing, like Caliban, to lick his feet. Easily distracted by the "glistering apparel" that will be his if he becomes king, Stephano fails to see the reality of their precarious situation. It is Caliban who reminds Stephano that "we shall lose our time" if Prospero awakes.

Inheriting the island from Sycorax, his mother, Caliban had

been his own king before Prospero came. As lord of it, Caliban had been free to roam the whole island then, and he does not associate his sovereignty of the natural world around him with costly royal robes. Born on the island, Caliban is the natural man who looks at Prospero's wardrobe as "trash" and cannot understand why Stephano and Trinculo "dote thus on such luggage." Stephano threatens to turn him out of his kingdom, however, if he does not assist them in their thievery.

Study Questions

1. Where has Ariel led Caliban, Stephano, and Trinculo with his tabor and pipe?

2. What does Prospero instruct Ariel to do in this scene?

3. What does Prospero call Caliban in this scene?

4. Why does Prospero feel he has treated Caliban humanely?

5. How do Stephano and Trinculo react to Prospero's expensive wardrobe?

6. How does Caliban react to Prospero's finery?

7. What have Stephano and Trinculo lost in the "filthy-mantled pool"?

8. What do Stephano and Trinculo do with Prospero's kingly robes?

9. Who carries the stolen clothing? Why?

10. What finally happens to the thieving trio?

Answers

1. Ariel has led the three conspirators into the "filthy-mantled pool."

2. Prospero tells Ariel to hang his royal wardrobe on the lime tree outside his cell.

3. Prospero calls Caliban a "born devil."

4. Prospero has taken Caliban into his own cell and taught him language.

5. Stephano and Trinculo are distracted, forgetting about their conspiracy to murder Prospero.

6. Caliban thinks Prospero's robes are nothing but "trash."

7. Stephano and Trinculo have lost their bottle of wine in the "filthy-mantled pool."

8. Stephano and Trinculo steal Prospero's robes.

9. Caliban is told that he must carry the stolen clothes or Stephano will turn him out of his kingdom.

10. The thieving trio is driven out by Prospero's spirits in the shape of dogs.

Suggested Essay Topics

1. Prospero says that Caliban is a "born devil, on whose nature/ Nurture can never stick." Explicate this passage in the light of Prospero's attempt at educating and civilizing Caliban. Why does Prospero feel it is an impossible task? What have been Prospero's frustrations when he thought he was treating him humanely? Is Caliban's nature evil because he is not civilized? How does he compare to Stephano and Trinculo who are civilized transplants on the island? Cite examples from the play to support your argument.

2. Stephano is unduly impressed with the finery of Prospero's wardrobe. Write an essay explaining Stephano's illusions in regard to his future kingship on the island. What illusions does Caliban have about Stephano? Is Trinculo opposed to Stephano as his king? Why does Trinculo imagine Stephano in Prospero's royal robes? What is Caliban's image of an ideal king on the island? Explain your answer with examples from the play.

SECTION SIX

Act V

Act V, Scene 1, lines 1-87

Summary

Act V opens with Prospero's declaration that the final resolution of his project is at hand. Ariel informs him the time is approaching the sixth hour when Prospero had promised their work would end. Ariel apprises him of the condition of the king and his followers, reporting that they are still confined, by Prospero's magic, to the grove of trees that acts as a windbreak to his cell. Alonso, Sebastian, and Antonio are completely distraught and the rest, particularly Gonzalo, can do nothing but mourn for them. Ariel is sure Prospero would sympathize with them in their afflictions if he could see them now. Prospero concedes that if Ariel, who is only air, has even a hint of feeling for them, surely he, who is human, would be more sympathetic to his own kind. Though he has been hurt by their "high wrongs," Prospero is ready to forgive them now if they are penitent. He instructs Ariel to release them, and he will break the magic spell and restore them to their senses.

After Ariel leaves, Prospero uses his staff to draw a magic circle on the ground. In a soliloquy he addresses the elves, demi-puppets, and fairies whose help he has engaged to perform such magic as dimming the noonday sun, calling forth the wind, thunder, and lightning, plucking up trees, and raising people from the dead. Ready now to renounce his magic, Prospero declares that he will break his magic staff, burying it far under the earth, and drop his magic book into the deepest region of the sea.

Ariel enters, ushering the frantic king and his royal court into Prospero's magic circle where they are held spellbound. Prospero has called for some "heavenly music" to soothe and comfort them in their present state of confusion. As the magic slowly wears off, their minds begin to develop a clearer comprehension of their surroundings. Prospero addresses Gonzalo, his "true preserver," assuring him that when they arrive home he will be fully rewarded for his past loyalty to him. He rebukes Alonso for his cruelty to him and his daughter and censures Sebastian for being an accomplice in the crime. Without remorse, Antonio, Prospero's own flesh and blood, has conspired with Sebastian to kill their king. Prospero promises forgiveness in spite of their unnatural deeds. Thus far none of the royal party has recognized Prospero, so he decides to remove his magician's robe and reveal his true identity as the former Duke of Milan.

Analysis

In the beginning of the scene, Ariel reminds Prospero that they are approaching the sixth hour when "you said our work should cease." This is a reminder of their conversation in Act 1 when Prospero "first raised the tempest." Ariel and Prospero are discussing the time of day which is "past the mid season/ At least two glasses" (2:00 o'clock). Prospero warns Ariel that "the time 'twixt six and now/ Must by us both be spent most preciously" (Act I, Scene 2, lines 240-41). As was noted elsewhere in the text, Shakespeare was observing the Aristotelian unity of time in which the action of the play takes place within the timespan of one day. Anxiously awaiting his freedom from his servitude to Prospero, Ariel reminds him that the time is running out.

Commentators have long recognized the Christian theological concept of sin and suffering followed by repentance, forgiveness, and reconciliation as an inherent idea in *The Tempest*. In Act III Alonso, Sebastian, and Antonio, cognizant of their sins, are warned by Ariel that repentance is their only means of escaping further doom. At that point in the play, Alonso acknowledges his sin against Prospero and feels he is suffering because he is to blame for his son's supposed death. The thunder "did bass my trespass./ Therefore my son in the ooze is bedded" (Act III, Scene 3, lines 99-

100). He has, however, not yet reached an awareness of the need for repentance but entertains thoughts of suicide instead. It is not until later (Act V, Scene 1) when Prospero decides that "the rarer action is/ In virtue than in vengeance" that the scene is set for forgiveness and repentance in the play. It has been debated that perhaps Prospero himself needed to make the conclusive choice between "virtue" and "vengeance" before Alonso could be truly repentant. Whatever the case may be, the Christian principle of redemption through repentance and forgiveness would have been a universally recognized truth to the audiences in Shakespeare's day and has been carried over to our modern times as well.

In Prospero's speech beginning with "Ye elves of hills," he invokes the elves, demi-puppets, and fairies to fill the air with some "heavenly music" which will assist him in working his "end upon their senses that/ This airy charm is for." Prospero repeatedly uses music to usher in his magic powers. He refers to the "solemn air," or song, as a comforter to the king and his royal court in their demented condition. Prospero then announces to his airy spirits that after this last act of magic in which he will forgive his enemies and restore his dukedom in Milan, he will abjure this "rough magic" by breaking his staff and drowning his book. His reference to "rough magic" is noteworthy since it leans toward the "black magic" of the foul witch Sycorax whose evil powers he has condemned earlier in the play. It is common knowledge that Prospero's speech contains ideas and language from Ovid's *Metamorphoses*. One of Medea's powers, for example, was to open graves and raise people from the dead. Sisson feels that "Shakespeare has been unwary in his borrowing from Ovid, and has read too much of Medea into Prospero's speech" (C. J. Sisson, *The Magic of Prospero*, 76). Much of Prospero's speech conflicts with his past adherence to his so-called "white magic." In referring to Prospero's spirits as "weak masters," Shakespeare was, perhaps, attempting to moderate the evil connotations of Prospero's strong magical powers in this scene.

In abjuring his magic, Prospero vows that he will bury his magic staff far beneath the earth, "and deeper than did ever plummet sound/ I'll drown my book." This is reminiscent of another passage where Alonso, grieving the loss of his son, vows that he will "seek him deeper than e'er plummet sounded/ And with him there

lie bedded" (Act III, Scene 3, ll. 101-2). The idea of the two passages is comparable, as is the obvious verbal imagery. Alonso's death is associated with the death of Prospero's magic. He must relinquish his magic if he hopes to regain his dukedom in Milan.

Study Questions

1. In what way is Shakespeare observing the Aristotelian unity of time?

2. Where has Ariel left the members of the royal party?

3. What is the emotional condition of the king and his followers?

4. What does Prospero decide to do about the royal party?

5. Why does Prospero call on his elves and fairies?

6. What does Prospero intend to do with his magic staff and book?

7. Why does Prospero give up his magic?

8. Why do the king and his royal party stand in a circle?

9. What does Prospero tell Alonso, Sebastian, and Antonio after the magic spell wears off?

10. What does Prospero do with his magic robe after he forgives his enemies?

Answers

1. The action of the play takes place within the timespan of one day.

2. Ariel has left the royal party imprisoned in a grove of trees next to Prospero's cell.

3. Alonso, Sebastian, and Antonio are distraught and the others are mourning for them.

4. Prospero intends to forgive the "three men of sin" if they are penitent.

5. Prospero calls on his elves and fairies to bring on some music for his next magical project.

6. Prospero will break his staff and throw his book into the sea.

7. Prospero's magic has accomplished its purpose of bringing his enemies to repentance and regaining his dukedom in Milan.

8. Prospero's magic circle keeps the king and his royal party spellbound.

9. Prospero tells the three men that they are forgiven for all their evil deeds.

10. Prospero removes his magic robe to present himself as the former Duke of Milan.

Suggested Essay Topics

1. *The Tempest* is often interpreted in the light of the Christian theological concept of sin followed by repentance and forgiveness. Write an essay explaining this concept as it applies to Alonso's sin and suffering and Prospero's consequent forgiveness. What has been Prospero's sole purpose for his actions toward Alonso thus far in the play? Is Alonso aware of his sin? Is he sorry for what he has done? How does his attitude reflect the Christian concept of sin? Cite examples from the play to explain your answer.

2. Prospero's "rough magic" in his speech abjuring magic conflicts with the image of "white magic" portrayed in the play thus far. Write an essay in which you compare and contrast the magic in the play so far with his description of his magic in this scene. In what way did Shakespeare's borrowings from Ovid influence the description? Have we seen Prospero dim the sun? Have we seen him call forth the winds? Why was his magic "rough"? Give examples from the play to support your argument.

Act V, Scene 1, 88-171

Summary

Prospero has taken off his magician's robe so that the king and his royal party will be able to recognize him as the former Duke of Milan. After he disrobes, he promises Ariel that he will soon be free. While Ariel helps to attire Prospero in his duke's clothing, he sings his freedom song. Identifying with the bee that gets its nectar from the flowers of the fields, he looks forward to his freedom when he will live "merrily" in the summer, making his home "under a blossom" hanging on the bough. Prospero tells him he will be missed, but he will, nevertheless, be given his freedom. Ariel is then instructed to remain invisible as he hurries to the king's ship to bring back the master and the boatswain who will be awake. He will, however, find the mariners asleep under the hatches. Ariel cheerfully tells him he will be back before his pulse beats twice.

Prospero then reveals himself to the king as the "wronged Duke of Milan." To prove he is really alive, he embraces Alonso and then Gonzalo and bids the others welcome. Filled with regret for his past deeds, Alonso immediately asks his forgiveness and restores his rightful title as the Duke of Milan. He wonders, however, how Prospero could possibly be alive and what he is doing here on this island. In an aside to Sebastian and Antonio, Prospero warns them that he could tell the king they are traitors, but, for now, he will remain silent. Cold and unrepentant, Sebastian simply replies that the devil speaks through Prospero. The former duke condemns his wicked brother Antonio but still forgives all of his faults. Though he requires his brother to restore his dukedom, Prospero knows he cannot do otherwise. Still puzzled, Alonso requests that Prospero relate the story of his survival this past 12 years and how he met them here on this island.

Alonso is suddenly reminded of the irreparable loss of his son Ferdinand, and Prospero consoles him with the news that he has also lost a daughter. Alonso responds spontaneously with the wish that his son and Prospero's daughter were both living in Naples as king and queen, and he could take his son's place at the bottom of the sea.

Prospero then notices the astonishment of the royal court who still cannot believe he is actually alive. He assures them he is Prospero who was deposed from Milan and landed on this island "to be the lord on't." He changes the subject since his story is too long to be told in one day and inappropriate for their first meeting. He invites the king to step into his cell which is his royal court, though he has few attendants and no subjects on the rest of the island.

Analysis

Ariel's song, "Where the Bee Sucks," functions to lift the action out of the present and into a world of freedom beyond the play. For Ariel that will not be the "brave new world" of Milan and Naples as the masque song suggests but the natural world instead. The tone of the song is joyful, but "dainty Ariel" does not display the unrestrained raucousness that Caliban does in his freedom song. Ariel's song exudes a joyfulness that comes from a well-earned freedom and demonstrates a restraint that is lacking in Caliban's song. The joyful, lazy freedom of summertime is suggested in the imagery. Ariel happily identifies with the bee that sucks nectar from the flowers and sleeps in a cowslip at night when the owls are hooting. A cowslip is a primrose with fragrant yellow flowers common to cow pastures in the sixteenth century. "Merrily, merrily" demonstrates Ariel's joyfulness at the prospect of freedom.

Ariel's future freedom on the island leads us to consider the future political world of Milan and Naples. The carefree, ideal world of eternal summer that the song portrays is a natural freedom that only spirits can possess, but for the leaders of Milan and Naples responsibility and freedom go hand in hand. Though Alonso, through his suffering, has now become repentant of his sins against Prospero and has willingly restored his dukedom, all the leaders must learn from their political mistakes of the past and take responsible action in the future if they are to maintain a sense of order. Ariel has warned the "three men of sin" earlier that their repentance must include "a clear (or sinless) life ensuing" (Act III, Scene 3, l. 82). When we consider their past record of governmental corruption and their obsession with their own power, even to the point of attempted murder of their fellow accomplices, Prospero's "brave new world" seems, somehow, fraught with uncertainty.

Recognizing his guilt, Alonso is purified or regenerated through repentance, and, consequently, reconciliation with Prospero follows, but for Antonio and Sebastian there is no repentance and no similar reconciliation. When Prospero censures them for their plot

against the king, Sebastian can only respond with "the devil speaks in him." Though Prospero forgives his brother Antonio for the usurpation of his dukedom, he condemns him in the same breath. "For you, most wicked sir, whom to call brother/ Would even infect my mouth, I do forgive/ Thy rankest fault - all of them." Antonio, and Sebastian have already opted to be excluded from the new order that is being established in Milan and Naples.

Alonso's deep regret for his son's death and his desire for reconciliation is seen in his response to Prospero's comment that he too has lost a daughter. With spontaneous enthusiasm Alonso expresses his wish that his son and Prospero's daughter could be king and queen of Naples, and that he, remembering his past sin against Prospero, could be "mudded in that oozy bed" where his son now lies. With Alonso's willingness to unite the two families politically, Prospero has accomplished his purpose in bringing the young couple together and is now ready to reunite father and son.

Study Questions

1. What is Ariel doing while he is singing?

2. Where will Ariel go when Prospero sets him free?

3. How does Ariel feel while he is singing his song?

4. How does Ariel's freedom song compare to Caliban's freedom song?

5. What does Alonso say when he sees Prospero?

6. How does Prospero assure Alonso and Gonzalo that he is still alive?

7. What does Prospero say to his brother Antonio?

8. What is Alonso's irreparable loss?

9. What does Alonso say that would reconcile him to Prospero and bring their families together?

10. What is Prospero ready to do in response to Alonso's wish for their children?

Answers

1. Ariel is helping to attire Prospero in his duke's clothing.

2. Ariel will stay on the island and live among the flowers.

3. Ariel feels happy because he will soon be free.

4. Ariel's freedom song is one of restrained joy and Caliban's song exhibits unrestrained raucousness.

5. Alonso asks Prospero's forgiveness for plotting the usurpation of Prospero's dukedom.

6. Prospero hugs Alonso and Gonzalo to prove he is still alive.

7. Prospero rebukes his brother Antonio and forgives him in the same breath.

8. The death of Alonso's son Ferdinand is an irreparable loss.

9. Alonso wishes that his son and Prospero's daughter would be king and queen of Naples.

10. Prospero is ready to reunite Alonso with his son Ferdinand.

Suggested Essay Topics

1. Ariel's song "Where the Bee Sucks" is a freedom song. Write an essay in which you compare and contrast Ariel's song to that of Caliban. In what way are they alike? How do both songs relate to Prospero? In what way are the songs different? What is the tone of each song. Cite examples from the play to explain your view.

2. Alonso expresses his wish that his son and Prospero's daughter would be king and queen of Naples. Write an essay addressing the political implications of Alonso's statement. In what way will it affect Prospero's new world in Milan? Why is Prospero ready to reunite Ferdinand and Alonso? How will Ferdinand and Miranda's marriage affect the political world of Milan and Naples? Give examples from the play to support your view.

Act V, Scene 1, 172-255

Summary

As Prospero pulls aside the curtain to the opening of his cave, he discloses Ferdinand and Miranda pretending to play chess but engaging in a lovers' conversation instead. Alonso thinks they are a vision of the island, and even Sebastian sees it as a "most high miracle" that Ferdinand has at last been found. When Ferdinand sees his father alive, he realizes that the threatening sea is merciful after all. Miranda is impressed with the handsome men of the royal court who come from the "brave new world" that she and Ferdinand will soon inhabit. Prospero simply replies that all this is new to her.

Alonso then inquires about Miranda whom Ferdinand could not have known for more than three hours. Ferdinand tells Alonso that he chose her to be his wife before he knew that he had a father who could have advised him. She is the daughter of the Duke of Milan about whom he has heard so much. Alonso knows he has sinned against Miranda as well as against her father. Realizing that Miranda will now be his daughter-in-law, Alonso is concerned about how it will sound for a father to ask forgiveness of his own child, but Prospero stops him, telling him not to dwell on past remembrances. Gonzalo invokes the gods to bless the young couple. He rejoices that in only one voyage, Alonso's daughter, Claribel, found her husband in Tunis; Ferdinand found a wife, Prospero found his dukedom; and they all found their true identity on this poor island. Alonso takes the hands of the young couple and pronounces a blessing upon them.

Ariel then enters with the Master and Boatswain. When Gonzalo sees the Boatswain, he immediately remembers that he has prophesied during the tempest that this blasphemous sailor was born to be hanged and would, therefore, not drown at sea if the gallows were on land. The Boatswain brings news that the ship is as good as new. Ariel reminds Prospero that he has done it all. Puzzled at the Boatswain's strange news, Alonso is convinced that these events are unnatural and asks him how he arrived at Prospero's cell. The Boatswain tells him he cannot remember since he had been asleep and was still in a daze when they were brought to this place. Ariel again seeks his master's approval for his actions, and Prospero assures him he will be set free.

Prospero consoles Alonso, still perplexed about the strange happenings, by telling him that soon the mystery will be solved. Until then, he encourages Alonso to remain cheerful. Prospero calls on Ariel to free Caliban and his companions and bring them to his cell. He apprises Alonso of the fact that there are still several members of his party who are missing.

Analysis

When Ferdinand sees that his father is alive, he immediately turns his thoughts to the image of the sea that "threatens" but is "merciful." Just as the sea has supposedly taken Ferdinand's father from him, it has mercifully brought him back and changed him as well. In "Full Fadom Five" Ariel sings his song about Ferdinand's "drown'd father." The song functions to inform Ferdinand that his father has not faded but "doth suffer a sea-change" (Act I, Scene 2, l. 401) which is symbolic of Alonso's suffering over the loss of his son, and his subsequent recognition of his sin against Prospero, leading to his repentance. By Act V Alonso's suffering has brought about a change that has quelled his inner tempest, relieving him of his guilt and bringing about his reconciliation with Prospero.

Alonso is now ready to meet Miranda and ask her forgiveness, though he is concerned and somewhat embarrassed by it. He is, after all, the king, and, through her marriage to Ferdinand, Miranda will be his child. According to the sixteenth-century law of "degree" and belief in the hierarchy of all beings, Alonso would be asking forgiveness of someone beneath his station in life which would be a threat to the natural harmony and, therefore, unacceptable. "O how oddly will it sound that I/ Must ask my child forgiveness." This is reminiscent of King Lear, a foolish old king who also asks his daughter's forgiveness for his injustice to her. "You must bear with me./ Pray you now forget, and forgive; I am old and foolish" (*King Lear*, Act IV, Scene 7, ll. 83-4). Like Alonso, Lear goes through great suffering before he arrives at repentance for his past deeds.

Miranda's innocent enthusiasm for the "goodly creatures" in the "brave new world" she will soon inhabit is immediately cut short by Prospero's remark which borders on cynicism, " 'Tis new

to thee." Having seen only three men (if Caliban can be included) in her lifetime, Miranda is not aware, as Prospero is, that among them are conspirators who have been willing to murder their own brothers for the sake of political power. Miranda demonstrated similar enthusiasm when she first saw Ferdinand as "a thing divine, for nothing natural/ I ever saw so noble" (Act I, Scene 2, ll. 18-19). Through their marriage, Ferdinand and Miranda look to a future "brave new world," however, with a vision of a new order established by those who have been redeemed through repentance and reconciliation.

At this point in the play, Gonzalo pulls all the threads of the action together in his expression of joy.

> In one voyage
> Did Claribel her husband find at Tunis,
> And Ferdinand, her brother, found a wife
> Where he himself was lost, Prospero, his dukedom
> In a poor isle; and all of us, ourselves,
> When no man was his own.

Though the characters have not all been purified or regenerated, at least their delusions have been shattered. In that sense they have, as Gonzalo says, all found themselves.

Study Questions

1. What are Ferdinand and Miranda pretending to do as Prospero discovers them? What are they really doing?

2. What does Ferdinand do when he sees his father, the king?

3. Why does Ferdinand feel that the seas are merciful?

4. What does Miranda think when she first sees the members of the royal court?

5. How does Alonso feel about asking Miranda's forgiveness?

6. How will Ferdinand and Miranda's marriage change the future "brave new world" of Milan?

7. How does Gonzalo react when he sees the boatswain?

8. What has happened to the ship in the tempest?

9. What does Prospero promise Ariel as a reward for his services?

10. Why is the boatswain unsure when Alonso asks him how he came to Prospero's cell?

Answers

1. Ferdinand and Miranda are pretending to play chess but are really engaging in loving conversation.

2. Ferdinand kneels before his father when he first sees him.

3. Symbolically, Ferdinand feels the seas are merciful because they have not drowned his father.

4. Miranda is impressed because there are so many noble men in the world.

5. Alonso is concerned about asking his own child's forgiveness since he is, by Elizabethan standards, superior to her.

6. The young couple's marriage will bring their fathers together and reconcile their past differences.

7. Gonzalo feels his prophecy has come true in which he vowed that the boatswain was born to be hanged and would, therefore, not drown at sea.

8. The ship is safely docked in the harbor and looks as good as new.

9. Prospero promises Ariel his freedom when his project is completed.

10. The boatswain had been asleep and was still in a daze when Ariel brought him to Prospero's cell.

Suggested Essay Topics

1. When Ferdinand meets his father, he regrets having cursed the sea since he now realizes that it is, after all, merciful. Explicate Ferdinand's words in the light of Prospero's "sea-change" in "Full Fadom Five." Why is Alonso's supposed

death symbolic of his change on the island? In what way is the tempest symbolic of Alonso's inner struggle? In what way has Alonso changed? What is Prospero's role in Alonso's change? Cite examples from the play to support your answer.

2. Miranda expresses an exuberance for all the "goodly creatures" who are part of the "brave new world" that she will soon inhabit with Ferdinand. Write an essay explaining the changes that will, hopefully, take place in the future world of Italy. What is the basis for the change? Do all the leaders share in the new hope for a world of peace and reconciliation? How will Sebastian and Antonio fit into this "brave new world"? Use examples from the play to support your argument.

Act V, Scene 1, 256-330

Summary

With Ariel in pursuit, Caliban, Stephano, and Trinculo, arrayed in Prospero's finery, appear to the men of the royal court. Stephano, too drunk to get his words straight, calls to his partners to shift for themselves. Trinculo thinks the king and his party are "a goodly sight," but Caliban is afraid Prospero will chastise him, though he is impressed when he sees his master in a duke's robe.

Sebastian and Antonio immediately see Caliban as a deformed fish-like monster, a marketable product to take back to Italy. Prospero informs Alonso and his royal court that Stephano and Trinculo have robbed him, and that Caliban, the son of an evil witch, has been plotting with them to take the duke's life. Seeing that Stephano and Trinculo are drunk, Alonso wonders where they got the liquor and why they are in this predicament. Sebastian greets Stephano with a pat on his back, but he shrugs him off, telling him he is no longer Stephano. Prospero reminds him that he had professed to be the future king of the island, but Stephano admits he would have been a poor one. Prospero admonishes Caliban, ordering him to take his companions to his cell to return the stolen clothing if he wishes to be pardoned for his evil deeds. Caliban recognizes his mistakes and promises to "seek for grace"

after this. He now understands the absurdity of taking "this drunk-ard for a god."

Prospero then invites Alonso and his royal train to his cell where they will rest for one night. Part of that time will be spent relating the events that have taken place in the lives of Prospero and Miranda since they left Milan 12 years ago. In the morning they will all be brought to the ship that will take them back to Naples where they will celebrate the marriage of Ferdinand and Miranda. Prospero promises them calm seas and favorable wind conditions for their trip. In an aside Prospero apprises Ariel of his final duty which is to provide fair weather for their sailing vessel. Bidding Ariel farewell, Prospero sets him free. He then turns to Alonso and his party and invites them into his cell. In the "Epilogue," Prospero, whose magic power is now gone, asks the audience to release him from the island, which has been the stage.

Analysis

By the end of the play, Alonso's suffering has brought him through the process of regeneration with an awareness of his sin and guilt and his subsequent repentance which is followed by Prospero's forgiveness. When Alonso restores Prospero's dukedom and accepts the marriage of his own son to Prospero's daughter, his change, evident in his reconciliation with Prospero, is finally complete. Conversely, Antonio and Sebastian, though they become acquiescent at the end, do not heed Ariel's earlier warnings of re-pentance to the "three men of sin." Unlike Alonso, neither of them has seen the error of his ways, and they both remain unrepentant. The ramifications of their choice and its effects on the future "brave new world" can be nothing more than mere conjecture, reaching beyond the world of the play. When we consider Antonio and Sebastian's reputation of conspiracy and murder, however, we are tempted to be dubious about the success of the new order being established in Milan and Naples.

Even Caliban, though he remains outside of the society of the redeemed, decides he will "be wise hereafter, / And seek for grace." He has learned his lesson, realizing the illusion he had been under when he took "this drunkard for a god." Prospero's pardon is given with the stipulation that Caliban and his friends return their stolen apparel to his cell. Though Caliban is, perhaps, eager to please his master because he is afraid he will be "pinch'd to death," he has also learned that his god who "bears celestial liquor" has clay feet after all.

Antonio sees Caliban as a "plain fish, and no doubt marketable." This is reminiscent of another reference to Caliban as a fish in Act II when Stephano decides that "if I can recover him, and keep him tame, I will not take too much for him; he shall pay for him that hath him, and that soundly" (Act II, Scene 2, ll. 76-8). Both passages allude to the practice in sixteenth-century Europe of exhibiting what they referred to as fish-like monsters in booths at the fair and charging admission.

Ariel finally gains his freedom through his release "to the elements" at the end of the play. His freedom beyond the play will exclude his songs since their function has generally been to further Prospero's designs which were to bring his enemies to repentance and ultimately achieve the restoration of his dukedom. Ariel's music will consist of the natural "noises, sounds, and sweet airs" (Act III, Scene 2, ll. 135-6) of the island that will function only for his delight in his ideal world of nature.

Prospero looks forward to the marriage of Ferdinand and Miranda in Naples where their union will symbolize the love that is the only hope for a new order. The reconciliation between the fathers, Alonso and Prospero, which has already taken place on the island, will be strengthened with the union of their children.

The "Epilogue" is Prospero's appeal to his audience to release him, with their applause, from the illusory world of the island or the imaginary world of the stage. His power is gone, his strength is faint, and he is asking the audience to clap their hands which will, metaphorically, create a "gentle breath" or breeze for the sails of his ship that will carry him to Naples. Their applause will break the imaginary spell of the play and release him to the real world of Naples which is symbolic of the real world of the audience.

Study Questions

1. Interpret Stephano's confused speech when he says, "Every man shift for all the rest, and let no man take care for himself."

2. How does Antonio react when he sees Caliban?

3. Do Antonio and Sebastian become repentant for their past deeds?

4. Does Caliban change in the course of the play?

5. Where will Ferdinand and Miranda celebrate their marriage?

6. Where will the king and his royal court spend the night?

7. How will Prospero entertain his overnight guests?

8. Who will make sure the royal party has calm seas for their trip to Naples?

9. Where does Ariel go when Prospero gives him his freedom?

10. What is the purpose of the "Epilogue"?

Answers

1. Stephano's speech refers to the proverbial "Let every man shift for himself."

2. Antonio sees him as a fish-like monster who can be sold for the purpose of exhibition to the public.

3. Antonio and Sebastian are not repentant, though they are no longer conspiring against Alonso.

4. Caliban realizes he has been under the illusion that he was mistaking a "drunkard for a god" and vows to "seek for grace" from now on.

5. Ferdinand and Miranda will celebrate their marriage in Naples.

6. The king and his royal court will spend the night in Prospero's cell.

7. Prospero will entertain the king and his court by relating the events of his life for the past 12 years.

8. Ariel is in charge of keeping the weather mild and the seas calm.

9. Ariel is released "to the elements" on the natural world of the island.

10. The "Epilogue" is Prospero's speech asking the audience with their applause to free him from the illusory world of the island or the stage with their applause.

Suggested Essay Topics

1. At the end of *The Tempest*, Antonio and Sebastian remain unrepentant for their past deeds. Write an essay in which you state the ramifications of their unrepentant attitude in the light of the future new order being established in Milan and Naples. Will they continue to remain acquiescent? Will they cooperate with Prospero as the restored Duke of Milan? How will they accept Ferdinand and Miranda's marriage and the consequent union of the two families? Will the "brave new world" be one of peace and reconciliation? Cite examples from the play to support your argument.

2. In the "Epilogue" Prospero asks the audience to "release me from my bands/ With the help of your good hands./ Gentle breath of yours my sails." Explicate this passage in the light of Prospero's decision to become part of the real world of Milan again. How does the island compare to the stage? Explain the symbolism of the spell the audience holds over the actors. How does the world of Naples compare to the world of the island? In which world does the audience dwell? To explicate this passage use examples from the play.

Sample Analytical Paper Topics

The following paper topics are designed to test your understanding of the play as a whole and analyze important themes and literary devices. Following each question is a sample outline to help you get started.

Topic #1

In "Full Fadom Five" the image of Alonso's "sea-change" symbolizes the change he goes through on the island and reflects one of the central themes of the play which is repentance, forgiveness, and reconciliation. Write an essay tracing the progress of Alonso's "sea-change" as his suffering brings him to the realization of his sin and guilt and to his subsequent regeneration.

Outline

I. Thesis Statement: *Alonso who suffers a "sea-change" on the island as he mourns the loss of his children, reaches an awareness of his sin and guilt, and repents for his past deeds which lead him to a reconciliation with Prospero.*

II. Mourns the loss of his children.

    A. Mourns the supposed death of Ferdinand.

        1. Ferdinand was the heir to the throne.

        2.   Suffers the loss of his loving son.

   B. Regrets the loss of his daughter.

        1.   He has lost his daughter through her marriage to the King of Tunis.

        2.   She has moved so far away that he is afraid he will never see her again.

   C. Alonso becomes despondent.

        1.   He longs for sleep to shut out his thoughts.

        2.   He loses hope in his search for his son.

III. Reaches an awareness of his sin and guilt.

   A. Alonso becomes aware of his sin against Prospero.

        1.   His conspiracy with Antonio in the usurpation of Prospero's dukedom.

        2.   Prospero and Miranda were left to die at sea.

        3.   Ariel appears, telling him to repent.

   B. Alonso becomes aware of his guilt for his son's death.

        1.   He feels his son's death is his punishment for his sin against Prospero.

        2.   He feels his son's death is his punishment for his sin against Miranda.

   C. Alonso entertains thoughts of suicide.

        1.   He longs to join his son at the bottom of the sea.

        2.   Symbolically, the sea will reunite father and son.

IV. Alonso's repentance and reconciliation.

   A. Asks Prospero to forgive his sin against him.

        1.   The sin of the usurpation of Prospero's dukedom.

        2.   Alonso's sin against Miranda.

        3.   Prospero forgives Alonso.

   B. Restore's Prospero's dukedom.

      1.   Alonso is regenerated as a result of his repentance.

      2.   He has lost his madness.

  C. Alonso accepts the marriage of his son to Prospero's daughter.

      1.   Is desirous of Miranda's forgiveness.

      2.   Wishes Ferdinand and Miranda were king and queen of Naples.

V. Conclusion: Alonso's "sea-change" is symbolic of the inner tempest that rages inside of him as he suffers a period of grief and loss, accompanied by despondency and thoughts of suicide. Because of Ariel's warning, Alonso becomes aware of his sin against Prospero which is followed by his repentance and Prospero's forgiveness. Alonso restores Prospero's dukedom and accepts the marriage of Ferdinand and Miranda which leads to his reconciliation with the former duke and makes his change on the island complete.

Topic #2

The Tempest is filled with music, containing more songs than any other Shakespearean play. Write an essay analyzing the function of the songs in the play in relation to theme, dramatic action, characterization, and the natural setting on the island.

Outline

I.   Thesis Statement: *The songs in The Tempest function for the purpose of assisting the dramatic action, delineating character, depicting themes, and lending atmosphere to the island.*

II. The songs assist the dramatic action.

  A. "Come Unto These Yellow Sands" and "Full Fadom Five" lead Ferdinand onto the island.

      1.   The song allays the tempest.

      2.   The song calms Ferdinand's passion concerning his drowned father.

  B. "While You Here Do Snoring Lie" moves the action along.

1. Wakes the sleepers, Alonso and Gonzalo.

2. Prevents the murder of the king and Gonzalo.

C. "Honor, Riches, Marriage-blessing," the masque song, lifts the action out of the play. Ferdinand and Miranda are shown their future life in Naples.

III. The songs delineate character.

A. "The Master, the Swabber, the Boatswain and I" delineates Stephano's character.

1. Stephano represents uninhibited sensuality.

2. Stephano embodies discord on the island.

B. "Where the Bee Sucks" delineates Ariel's character.

1. Ariel is "dainty."

2. Ariel is a natural being of the island.

C. "No More Dams I'll Make for Fish" delineates Caliban's character.

1. Caliban is a raucous natural man.

2. Caliban is a "howling monster."

IV. The songs depict themes of the play.

A. "Full Fadom Five" depicts the theme of Alonso's "sea-change."

1. Through suffering Alonso recognizes his sin, repents, is forgiven and is regenerated.

2. Metaphorically, the "sea-change" represents Alonso's change throughout the play.

B. "Where the Bee Sucks" and "No More Dams I'll Make for Fish" depict the theme of freedom.

1. Caliban's freedom from Prospero's servitude.

2. Caliban's servitude to Stephano is an illusion.

3. Ariel is given a well-earned freedom at the end of the play.

C. "Honor, Riches, Marriage-blessing" depicts the theme of

hope for a future "brave new world."

1. The song promises a world based on love.

2. The song promises a world of pastoral abundance and fruition.

3. Together, Ferdinand and Miranda will kiss "the wild waves whist" or still the tempest of hatreds and political rivalries of the play.

V. The songs lend atmosphere to the island.

   A. An atmosphere of peace, tranquillity, and freedom from fear

      1. "Be not afeard, the isle is full of noises,/ Sounds, and sweet airs."

      2. "Come Unto These Yellow Sands" depicts a pastoral scene with dogs barking and roosters crowing.

   B. An atmosphere of beauty.

      1. "Where the Bee Sucks" depicts Ariel's world of cow slips, owls, and bats.

      2. "Full Fadom Five" depicts the sea with its beautiful pearl and coral.

VI. Conclusion: In *The Tempest* the songs are not mere "ditties" meant to entertain but function to assist the dramatic action, delineate character, depict themes, and lend an atmosphere of peace and natural tranquillity to the island. The songs are an artistic success in the play, adding beauty and functioning as an integral part of the poetic drama.

Topic #3

Shakespeare portrays Caliban as a natural man "on whose nature/ Nurture can never stick." Write an essay contrasting Caliban's nature to that of the civilized characters on the island as they interact with one another.

Outline

I. Thesis Statement: *Caliban, "a savage and deformed slave," is seen in stark contrast to the civilized characters in the play with regard to education, social mores, leadership, and a respect for nature.*

II. Contrast in Caliban and Miranda's education.

    A. Prospero has taught both Caliban and Miranda.

        1. Miranda benefits; she recognizes the nobility in Ferdinand and in the "goodly creatures" of her future "brave new world".

        2. Caliban was taught language, and his only benefit was that it taught him "how to curse."

    B. Educating Caliban was useless.

        1. "Good natures/ Could not abide to be with" Caliban.

        2. All efforts to educate him have been frustrated.

III. Contrast in Caliban and Ferdinand's social mores.

    A. In their relationship to Miranda.

        1. Caliban violates Miranda's honor.

        2. Ferdinand does not allow his honor to turn into lust.

    B. In their attitudes toward log-bearing.

        1. Caliban views it as punishment.

        2. Ferdinand bears logs in the service of his mistress.

IV. Contrast in Caliban and Prospero's leadership abilities

    A. Caliban has been his own king who inherited the island from the evil witch, Sycorax, his mother.

        1. Prospero arrives to be lord on it.

        2. Prospero takes Caliban as his slave.

    B. Caliban leads Stephano and Trinculo in a plot to kill Prospero.

        1. Caliban's plan is aborted.

        2. Caliban admits he had poor judgement in seeing Stephano as a god.

V.   Contrast in attitudes toward nature among Caliban and his fellow conspirators.

    A.   Caliban is unimpressed with the duke's royal clothing.

        1.   Thinks the royal robes are "trash".

        2.   Begs Stephano and Trinculo to stop doting on the duke's luggage.

    B.   Caliban is in tune with the music of the island.

        1.   Stephano and Trinculo are afraid of Ariel's music.

        2.   Caliban consoles his friends with "be not afeard, the isle is full of noises,/ Sounds, and sweet airs, that give delight and hurt not."

        3.   Caliban speaks the poetry of the island in verse.

        4.   Stephano and Trinculo speak in the prose given to servants.

VI. Conclusion: Caliban is the "natural man" of the island. He is portrayed as a savage who cannot benefit from the civilizing influence of Prospero's education which has only taught him "how to curse." He views Miranda as a natural female to be pursued and overtaken. Though he has been his own king on the island, his powers cannot match Prospero's sophisticated art. He is, however, in tune with the natural rhythms of the island which "give delight and hurt not."

SECTION EIGHT

Bibliography

Primary Sources

Shakespeare, William. *The Riverside Shakespeare,* ed. G. Blakemore Evans. Boston: Houghton Mifflin, 1974.

The First Folio of Shakespeare, The Norton Facsimile, ed. Charlton Hinman. New York: W. W. Norton, 1968.

Secondary Sources

Berger, Karol. "Prospero's Art," *Shakespeare Studies,* Vol. X. New York: Burt Franklin, 1977.

Coleridge, Samuel Taylor. *Shakespearean Criticism.* London: J. M. Dent and Sons, 1961.

Craig, Hardin. "Magic in *The Tempest," Philological Quarterly,* 47 (1968): 8-15.

Cutts, John P. *"The Tempest,* the Sweet Fruition of Revenge," *Rich and Strange.* Washington State University Press, 1968.

Dowden, Edward. Sha*kespeare: A Critical Study of His Mind and Art.* London: Routledge and Kegan Paul, 1875.

Dryden, John. "Prologue to *The Tempest," The Norton Anthology of English Literature,* Vol. 1. New York: W. W. Norton, 1968.

Frye, Northrop. *A Natural Perspective: The Development of Shakespearean Comedy and Romance.* New York: Columbia University Press, 1965.

Godschalk, William Leigh. *Patterning in Shakespearean Drama: Essays in Criticism.* University of Cincinatti: Mouton-The-Hague-Paris, 1973.

Johnson, Samuel. *Johnson's Notes to Shakespeare.* Los Angeles: William Andrews Clark Memorial Library, 1956.

Kermode, Frank. *The Arden Shakespeare, The Tempest.* London: Methuen, 1969.

Knight, G. Wilson. *The Crown of Life: Essays in Interpretation of Shakespeare's Final Plays.* London: Oxford University Press, 1947.

Long, John H. *Shakespeare's Use of Music.* Gainesville, Florida: University of Florida Press, 1961.

Lowell, James Russell. *The English Poets.* London: Kennikat Press, 1888.

Lovejoy, Arthur O. *The Great Chain of Being.* Cambridge, Massachusetts: Harvard University Press, 1950.

Nuttall, A. D. *Two Concepts of Allegory,* London: Routledge and Kegan Paul, 1967.

Sisson, C. J. "The Magic of Prospero," *Shakespeare Survey* II. London: Cambridge University Press, 1958.

Traversi, Derek. *Shakespeare: The Last Phase.* Stanford, California: Stanford University Press, 1969.

Virgil. *The Aeneid,* ed. Moses Hadas. London: Bantam Books, 1965.

Wright, Neil. "Reality and Illusion as a Philosophical Pattern in *The Tempest,*" *Shakespeare Studies,* Vol. X. New York: Burt Franklin, 1977.

Zimbardo, Rose A. "Form and Disorder in *The Tempest,*" *Shakespeare Quarterly,* 14 (1963): 49-56.